Walk Strathkelvin

Strathkelvin Ramblers

First published by Strathkelvin Ramblers 2002

ISBN 1 901184447

Maps reproduced from the Ordnance Survey map with the permission of Her Majesty's Stationery Office, © Crown Copyright NC/00/1288, November 2000

Rights of Way maps reproduced with the permission of the Scottish Rights of Way and Access Society

Editor: John Logan, Lenzie

Final typing by Ann Kaniuk, Milton of Campsie

Route sketch maps by Mike Shand, Milton of Campsie

Cover by Hawkeye Aerial Photography, Kirkintilloch

Printed by Deacon Brothers, Kirkintilloch

Published by Strathkelvin Ramblers, Kirkintilloch

Copies obtainable from Ottakar's Bookstore, Buchanan Galleries, Glasgow G1 2FF, 0141 353 1500. Price £6.99.

Acknowledgements

Walk Strathkelvin would not have been possible to produce without the willing voluntary work of the many people who devised, explored, described, typed, proof-read and proof-walked over seventy walks in Part One.

Members and friends of Strathkelvin Ramblers
Jean Addison, John Anderson, Freda and Jim Bunyan, Marion Campbell, Alan Connor, Ella Corbet, Stuart Dickson, Bill Findlay, Betty Gorman, Bob and Shirley Hepburn, Alex Imrie, Charles Kennedy, Jim Lawson, Tom Lochrie, Ewan, Kirsty and Ross Logan, Ian McCallum, Pat McGowan, Anne and Drew McNicol, Brenda Pate, Anne and Ron Paton, Jessie and Douglas Robertson, Eunice Russell, Penny Sinclair and John and Margaret Whitelaw.

Other organisations
Grateful thanks are also extendeded to Ally Corbett and Jackie Gillespie of Kelvin Valley Countryside Project, Catriona McDonald of East Dunbartonshire District Council, Bridget Jones of North Lanarkshire Council, Guthrie Hutton, Chairman of the Forth and Clyde Canal Society, Alistair Lawson of the Scottish Rights of Way and Access Society and Johan Gerrie of Scottish Natural Heritage

Strathkelvin Ramblers Committee
This authorised the project. Members: Stuart Dickson, Marjory Dunn, James King, James Lawson, John Logan, Iain McKinnon, Aileen McLay, Margaret Rutherford, Rena Scott and Penny Sinclair.

Editorial panel
Freda Bunyan, Stuart Dickson, Betty Gorman, Ewan Logan, Ian McCallum and John Whitelaw. Editor: John Logan.

Contents

Cover picture: Whitefield Pond, Lennoxtown

Foreword

It seems such a short time since I wrote the Foreword to *The First Five Years.*

That book described the activities of the Strathkelvin Ramblers, which I helped to found in 1992 and which grew to two hundred members in that time.

As it is now entering its tenth year of existence, I am pleased to be able to write the Foreword to the second book, *Walk Strathkelvin.*

This book is intended to encourage people of all ages and abilities to explore the local countryside on foot, over some seventy short walks of half an hour to half a day, and perhaps in the company of others to go further afield.

Here's to the next five years.

Happy walking!

Tom Weir

Introduction

As a youngster living on the south side of Glasgow I would often gaze from my classroom window out across the city to the blue rise of the Campsie Fells. At weekends my pals and I would catch a bus to places like Blanefield, Milton of Campsie and Lennoxtown, and we'd explore those high moors in all weathers, learning the rudiments of outdoor skills and birthing a life-long affinity with the hills.

We didn't know much about the byways of Strathkelvin – we were too anxious to reach the high tops – and in many ways that's been the story of my life, exploring further and further afield, not only in Scotland but also to the distant ranges of the world. And while travelling is great, it's also good to come home and learn something of the wonders that lie close to our very doorstep.

If I've learned anything in 25 years of writing about mountains and wild places, it's that you don't actually have to travel very far to experience the beauty and the miracle of nature. Following in the footsteps of the great John Muir in the high Sierra Nevada mountains of California is thrilling, but so is the realisation that on Glasgow's outskirts, near Lenzie, is a 10 000-year-old peat bog, complete with its own rarity, Bog Rosemary. The great ecologist would have been delighted to see it in its native setting.

Good to be reminded, too, that not far from the centre of Kirkintilloch Roman soldiers once stood guard against the fierce Caledonians, and that the infamous Comyn family, erstwhile contenders for the Scottish crown in medieval times, once had a stronghold here. The spirit of place, engendered by the events of history, is as alive here as it is in the wilder, further corners of our land. And this book will help you experience it for yourself.

There's a fine variety of walks and wanders here – there's history and wildlife and a rich vein of local knowledge running through all the route descriptions. As a guide to the byways and quiet ways of Strathkelvin this is a book that demands to be used – so reach out for your boots, grab your pack, and go. The delights of Strathkelvin await you…

Cameron McNeish
President, Ramblers' Scotland

Part One

About Part One

The walks in Part One, each taking from half an hour to half a day, explore the community council areas in the former Strathkelvin District, from Gartcosh in the south to the Campsies in the north. The social, economic and political history is described in a special article by Don Martin at the start of each area.

Some nature notes by Ian McCallum are included in the walk descriptions. These usually relate to when the walk was surveyed. Each month will have different aspects to interest the reader. Obviously, flowers will not bloom in the winter and the geese and redwing will not be evident in the summer. As many as possible of the footpaths and rights of way are followed. These paths are listed, mapped and maintained by the new District Councils –East Dunbartonshire and North Lanark.

Line drawings of the routes accompany the narratives. An indication of how to reach each start point by walking or by public transport is given. The last walk in each group leads to the start point of the next group. With the exception of Baldernock, each of the start points is accessible by public transport.

Railway lines from Glasgow Queen Street to Dunblane and Edinburgh go through Bishopbriggs, Lenzie and Croy. Those to Falkirk Grahamston and Cumbernauld go through Stepps (and perhaps one day through Gartcosh again). Bus routes from Glasgow Buchanan Bus Station go through Bishopbriggs, Kirkintilloch, Milton of Campsie and Lennoxtown to Clachan of Campsie; and through Stepps to Muirhead. Local services link Torrance with Kirkintilloch, Lenzie and Muirhead, and to Coatbridge by Gartcosh.

Operators, routes and timetables alter from time to time; it is advisable to check before travelling. Useful phone numbers are:
Scotrail 08457 484 950; SPT 0141 332 7133; Traveline 0870 608 2 608.

Safety note: Especially when walking on country roads with no footpaths, it is advisable to wear high-visibility clothing for safety reasons. 'See and be Seen'.

When walking, anything untoward observed, such as litter, dumping of rubbish, obstructions, or damage to signposts or stiles should please be notified to the relevant Community or District Council for remedial action. Addresses are listed at the end of Part One.

Community history – Don Martin

Gartcosh

The village of Gartcosh owes its existence to the steelworks that for so long dominated the local landscape. The works was established in 1865 on the north side of the Garnkirk & Glasgow Railway, by the firm of William Gray & Co. It was known at first as Woodneuk Iron Works, and indeed was then concerned with the production of malleable iron. Two rows of houses were constructed immediately adjacent to the works, for the accommodation of the ironworkers. To a large extent these houses were occupied by migrants from the Midlands of England, with a few from South Wales. Gartcosh was for many years notable for the number of English surnames in evidence.

In 1872 the works was taken over by the firm of Smith & McLean, under whose ownership it developed into an important steelworks. During the late 1890s and early 1900s Smith & McLean provided new brick-built houses for their workers in Lochend Road and plots immediately adjacent. Two of the terraces were named McLean Place and Smith Terrace, after the firm. Gartcosh Steelworks eventually passed into the ownership of Colvilles Ltd, who opened a cold reduction steel strip mill at Gartcosh in 1963, in conjunction with their larger operation at Ravenscraig, near Motherwell. Despite a high-profile campaign to save it, Gartcosh Strip Mill was eventually closed by the British Steel Corporation in 1986. By that date the former Smith & McLean houses in Lochend Road had already gone, replaced by a new housing development in the Mowbray Avenue/Eastgate vicinity.

Another important industry at Gartcosh was the fireclay works, established by James Binnie in 1863. Although mostly concerned with firebrick manufacture, during the early years its output was much more varied, extending to garden vases and pedestals, garden edges, fountains, chimney cans, roof tiles, cattle troughs, sewage pipes and other products. It was one of a group of such businesses in the area, with others at Cardowan, Garnkirk, Heathfield and Glenboig. Gartcosh Fireclay Works eventually closed down in the 1950s, when local supplies of fireclay were exhausted.

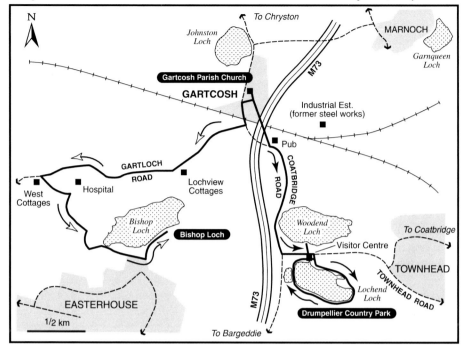

Gartcosh Parish Church
How to get there. Walk from Muirhead by Station Road, Drumcavel Road and Lochend Road (about an hour). Bus from Muirhead or Coatbridge.

Bishop Loch
About two hours

From the church turn right up Lochend Road and right again (shops on the right and a farm on the left). Turn left on to the main Muirhead to Coatbridge road and cross over. After a short distance turn right into Gartloch Road. The view of the hills is obstructed by containers stacked at the nearby terminal. Keep on past a group of two-storey houses on the left then Lochview Cottages and a heavily fenced driveway. The road bends to the right, soon reaching the west entrance to Gartloch Hospital. Keep on past more cottages and at the next row go left through a gate on to the remnants of one of the drives into the hospital grounds. Follow the track between iron railings to a fork, taking the right one. The ruins of flats (nurses' quarters?) can be seen on the left, and there is a view of the

3

buildings of Easterhouse to the right. The path now skirts the west end of the loch which is obscured by tall grass and reeds. Approaching some trees on the right, the path bends to the left. As the path rises, the view over the loch opens up. The path does not go right round the loch, although there are plans to extend it. At an entrance, marked by a stone horse and vehicle barrier, turn and go back by the same route to Gartcosh.

Bishop Loch SSSI

By Ally Corbett, of KVCP

Bishop Loch Local Nature Reserve (LNR) is one of the most important wetland sites in central Scotland, consisting of a diversity of habitat and providing a permanent or seasonal home for many species, especially birds. On this basis the loch is accorded protection from harmful activities by its designation as a Site of Special Scientific Interest.

Bishop Loch is also of geological interest, having been created some 10 000–15 000 years ago at the retreat of the last ice age, when huge blocks of ice were left behind. These sank into the underlying boulder clay and then slowly melted to form the loch. The first indications of human activity in the area date from the Early Iron Age with the discovery of a crannog, or man-made island dwelling, to the eastern end of the loch. In the Middle Ages the loch formed part of the Bishop of Glasgow's estates and at that time one could navigate by a series of waterways from Hogganfield Loch through Frankfield, Woodend and Johnstone Lochs to Bishop Loch. Development and encroaching vegetation mean that little evidence now remains of these waterways.

Agricultural practices and the planting of woodland to screen Gartloch Hospital have had a major impact on the landscape over the years. A more profound effect from the building of the hospital was the release of large amounts of sewage into the loch, raising the nutrient levels and resulting in a vast expansion of the reed beds, ironically one of the habitats that make the loch so important. The development of the housing estate has also had a dramatic effect on the loch and its environs, bringing with it many new pressures in the form of vandalism, shooting, fly tipping, grassland fires and generally detrimental disturbance to flora and fauna.

Apart from its value for wildlife, Bishop Loch provides an important "green lung" for the people of Easterhouse, and indeed those from further afield. With this in mind, Kelvin Valley Project has over the years undertaken substantial access work around the loch aimed at encouraging people to utilise the area for informal recreation and enjoyment of a wildlife-rich environment in an urban setting. This has taken the form of formalised access points and a network of paths which, whilst encouraging the public to use the loch, has steered them away from some of the more sensitive habitats.

Kelvin Valley has also been instrumental in the creation of new habitat around the loch with the planting of new sections of native woodland and the creation of a wild flower meadow. These were done in conjunction with local schools, first as an educational

4

tool and second in the hope that by involving local children in the improvement of their environment a sense of ownership could be instilled, resulting in less vandalism and damage to the loch. To complement the site work of the schools, and to tie in with the environmental education curriculum, Kelvin Valley produced a Bishop Loch Education Pack, which was distributed to all the local primary schools.

The ultimate aim for Bishop Loch, together with Hogganfield Loch LNR and Cardowan Moss, is to create a "North Glasgow Biodiversity Park", which will have continuity of paths, access and interpretation. To this end we are in the process of commissioning an Interpretation Strategy for the entire area, where the main focus will be community consultation and involvement and education.

Bishop Loch is a great asset to north-east Glasgow. Working in partnership with other interested parties, from residents' associations to SNH, we hope to continue its protection and enhancement and to encourage others to enjoy all that it has to offer.

Gartcosh to Drumpellier Country Park

About an hour and a half

From the church turn right up the main street, over a crossroads, down past the Community Hall and the Primary School and on to a path alongside the railwayline over the motorway. Keep on the path, which bends round to the left under the railway and merges with the old road through Gartcosh. Passing some houses and the Chapman Inn, the route joins the new road. Taking the pavement, go left, passing a road to the left at present signed to a riding school, but it is for sale so the sign may change. Pass another road to the left marked Woodend Farm. Take the next road to the left, well signposted for Drumpellier Country Park. The entrance is a short distance along on the right. Before going in, turn off the road to the left and along a short path to the edge of Woodend Loch, a haven for wildlife, to help protect which there is no path round the loch. Return to the road and cross into the park. The building houses the rangers, information and a café. Walkways go round the Lochend Loch and at the point farthest from the main building is a butterfly farm, open in the summer months.

Return to Gartcosh Church by the same route.

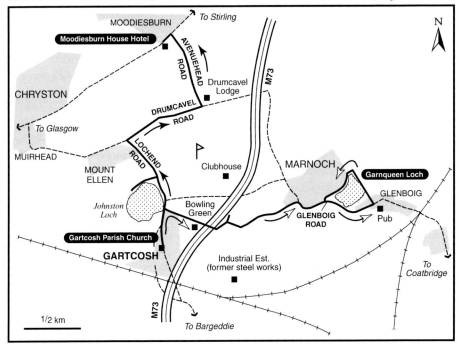

Garnqueen Loch via "Ducks' Walk"

About two hours

Start at Gartcosh Parish Church, and turn left along Lochend Road, which merges with the main Coatbridge to Chryston road leading back to the village, marked "local". Take the short footpath leading to the next exit from the roundabout and keep on the pavement leaving the next two roundabouts on the left. On the way can be seen new houses on the hill to the left, and on the right the bowling green and social club. The grounds seem to have benefited from the landscaping of the new road system. The bridge over the motorway is one of the highest points in a fairly flat area affording a good view: to the north the Campsies, to the south over Coatbridge to Tinto with a glimpse of the Cathkin Braes, and to the west the highrise flats of Glasgow. From the ridge looking down to the right, there is a triangle of ground bounded by roads with grass and trees and a bridleway for horse riding, indicated by the road signs.

After passing the third roundabout, cross the slip road to the new industrial park being created from the former Gartcosh steel works, presently used for the processing of old newspapers, collected in the familiar blue bags. There are plans for industrial development by Scottish Enterprise and North Lanark Council. The steel strip mill was a hive of industry, but when it was closed down, nature moved in with some surprising results. An area was suitable for amphibians, especially newts, and this caused a problem of a clash of interests: on the one hand, trying to encourage new industry to move into the area, and on the other, trying to maintain the biodiversity that had moved into the area. The green walls that can be seen are an attempt to move the life forms out of the development area and into more ecofriendly areas. The walls also minimise road casualties, as during breeding times frogs, toads and newts are vulnerable to being squashed on the road by vehicles. The walls tend to prevent the amphibians from crossing the road on the surface, and allow them to use mini-underpasses.

Now head down a newly created flight of steps and path, which is Ducks' Walk. Further information about this area may be obtained by reading the journal of the Glasgow Natural History Society, *The Glasgow Naturalist*, Volume 23, Part 6, 2001, pages 22–23: "An Unusual Assemblage of Plants at Gartcosh", by P. MacPherson.

The path goes through mature woodland with rhododendrons, possibly the grounds of a former estate. Along the path will be seen several native trees, including beech. The beech fruits only every three or four years, which is possibly an arrangement to reduce regular predation. In this country the mast is consumed avidly by squirrels and pigs. The fruit is small and difficult to harvest, but on the Continent its oil is used in salads or for frying or making butter.

After a line of concrete bollards, presumably to deter vehicles, several paths cross. Leave the first on the left which heads back to the motorway skirting the trees, and take the second on the left through the wood down to the Bothlin Burn, which is liable to flooding at this point. This may be a likely home for ducks, hence the name of the walk. Return to the main path, turn left and continue towards Glenboig. The young trees on the right are the remains of a large number purchased from the Glasgow Garden Festival for planting in parks throughout the district. The path becomes a cart track down to Glenboig Gardens at the Gartcosh to Glenboig road. Turn right on to the pavement of the road to Glenboig and keep going into the village. Just before reaching the Garnqueen Inn, there is a gap in the houses on each side of the road. This is the track of the dismantled railway from Glasgow to Coatbridge. Cross over the road to take the track to the left, and shortly arrive at Garnqueen Loch on the left. This is home to American ruddy duck with their distinctive blue beaks, all fiercely protected by the residents of the houses on the far side of the loch. Keep on the track to the houses and turn left to rejoin the road to Glenburn Gardens, and so back to Gartcosh Parish Church.

Gartcosh to Moodiesburn, via Johnston Loch

About an hour for the round trip

Start at the church, turn left along Lochend Road, crossing over the main road and keeping on northwards. There is no access to the loch either by the lane behind Loch View Terrace or in front – both are private. Soon, just after the roundabout, there is a well kept stretch of grass with the loch over to the left. Turn left on to a poorly surfaced road, which leads to and stops at a nursery. There is no way round the loch, but if you stop anywhere on the parkland or the side road, good views of the loch and the wildfowl may be had. The loch is used by a fishing club which was run originally by the Gartcosh steel strip mill. Unfortunately, the steel industry in Gartcosh has been axed with the attendant dereliction of the factory sites. On the loch can be seen tufted duck, coot, and the American ruddy duck which caused a minor political upheaval when the RSPB sanctioned the shooting of this species to prevent it hybridising with the rare white-headed duck in Spain.

Turn left in to Drumcavel Road and up the hill to Mount Ellen housing scheme and downhill, crossing the road and turning sharp right on to the road with the golf course on the right. There is no pavement. Soon the Bothlin Burn is crossed and the road goes uphill. Turn left at the first opportunity, downhill to where the Railway Walkway crosses. At the time of writing this leads to Strathblane to the left and does not continue to the right, but it may do so one day through Coatbridge, Bathgate and Edinburgh. Keep on the road, uphill and on to the traffic lights on the main Glasgow to Stirling road. Turn left on the pavement to the Moodiesburn Hotel, the starting point for Moodiesburn walks. Return by the same route to Gartcosh Church.

Community history – Don Martin

Moodiesburn

Moodiesburn first enters the history books as a stopping-place on the main stagecoach route between Glasgow and Stirling. In November 1805 the "New North Star Coaches" were advertised as running between Glasgow and Stirling "By Moodie's-burn and Lone head, Drawn by four able Horses, with careful Drivers and Guards". A few houses on the south side of the main road, just west of the crossroads, are all that remain of this phase of Moodiesburn history. The convenient roadside location of the Moodiesburn House Hotel also serves as a reminder of the village's role in former times.

On the northern fringes of Moodiesburn stood the mining village of Bridgend. It was built to provide homes for miners and other workers from the nearby Auchengeich Colliery, opened in 1905. The houses were mostly brick-built room-and-kitchen dwellings, with inside water-closet and scullery. A more primitive building on the site, the stone-built "White Row", was a survivor from an earlier era. There were 104 dwellings in total, also ten ash-bins and a similar number of wash-houses, for use of the residents. Decline set in after 1959, when a calamitous disaster at Auchengeich Pit curtailed its working life, and the houses were vacated during the 1960s, with final site clearance in 1967. All that survives of a once-thriving village is the Auchengeich Miners Welfare Institute and a memorial to the 47 Auchengeich disaster victims nearby.

Modern Moodiesburn is essentially a group of housing estates. First to be erected were the timber houses on the former Gartferry Estate, in the 1930s. Some wartime pre-fab houses were later demolished, but further extensive development took place during the post-war period. A small primary school at Bridgend soon proved inadequate and was superseded by the new schools of Glenmanor (in 1965) and St Michael's (in 1969). A hall for Church of Scotland worshippers was opened in Blackwood Crescent by Chryston Parish Church in 1969. St Michael's Roman Catholic Church was dedicated in 1966. The Pivot Community Education Centre was opened in 1976, together with the adjacent library.

A significant modern industry was established at Moodiesburn during 1964–65 when the sausage casing manufactory of Devro Ltd. was built and opened. This provided significant employment opportunities for the growing Moodiesburn population.

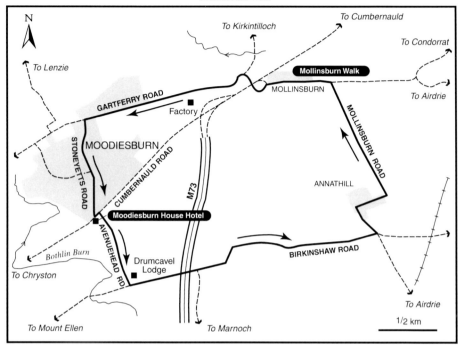

Moodiesburn House Hotel

How to get there. Walk from Gartcosh, as described. Bus from Glasgow or Kirkintilloch or Coatbridge via Gartcosh.

Moodiesburn House Hotel to Mollinsburn

About two and a half hours

On leaving the hotel turn right towards the lights and right again into Avenuehead Road, a country road. After a bit of a dip in the road, notice the track on the right. This is the Railway Walkway to Strathblane. At present it does not continue to Coatbridge to the left, as permission has not been obtained to go through a disused sand quarry. Keep going uphill and turn left at the T-junction into Drumcavel Road, with Drumcavel Lodge on the corner. This road goes under the motorway, and soon after on the right may be seen the continuation of the Walkway. The road continues through pleasant countryside.

One of the interesting things is a land development site on the left, formerly Bedlay Colliery. This is an area where there is a profusion of red and white clovers. There is another clover that looks similar and is called the alsike clover, but which has a white flower flushed pink below. In the hedgerows you can find ground elder, tufted vetch, hedge parsley, ladies' bedstraw, violets, spear thistle, hogweed, sticky willy, meadow vetchling, lesser stitchwort, knotweed and great hairy willowherb. Lime, beech, ash and larch are also to be found in the hedgerow. Adjacent to the road are marshy areas that are good for amphibians. Robins, wrens, house sparrows, crows and swallows are the common birds.

At the next T-junction with a large farm on the right, turn left for the village of Annathill through which the road bends right then left. Soon Mollinsburn can be seen on the left. At the next T-junction, before turning left, turn right uphill. At the top, where there is a new water installation, is a wonderful view of the surrounding countryside, Condorrat and Cumbernauld below, a glimpse of the Forth to the right, and the Campsie Fells ahead and to the left. Turn back downhill and go down to Mollinsburn village. Before you enter Mollinsburn on the right-hand side, there is a hillside covered with gorse and bramble and at the burnside feverfew grows abundantly. This plant was prescribed to treat infertility, assisting labour and preventing abortion. Where the road forks, bear left up and over the motorway, turning first left into Gartferry Road, which leads past the large sausage-casing factory into Moodiesburn. Before you reach the factory, on the left-hand side of the road, there is a marshy area that is good for wild flowers such as common spotted orchid and sneezewort. Several butterflies occur including the small tortoiseshell. The rushes that appear to be the common smooth rush are the rarer compact rush, which is identified by its close-knit flower head and ridged stem.

Turn left into Stoneyetts Road and so back to the lights and the hotel.

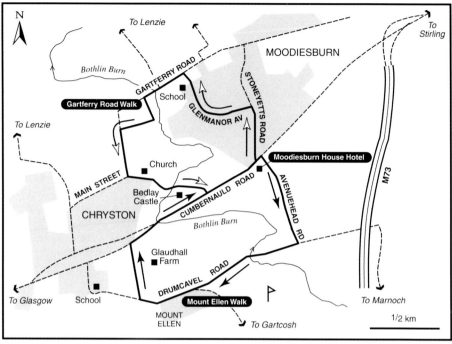

Moodiesburn House to Mount Ellen
About an hour

Leave the hotel, turn right and right again at the lights into Avenuehead Road. As you turn into Avenuehead Road there is an open sports field on the left that is a good area for watching birds feeding. Because it is an open space the birds feel safe, away from the bushes, etc., which could give cover to predators. Birds include rooks, crows, jackdaws, gulls (common, black-headed and lesser black-backed gulls), starlings, house sparrows and blackbirds. In the winter, redwing and fieldfare may be seen. As you progress up the road, there is good hedge cover including hawthorn, ash, elder, privet, nettle, bindweed, brambles and the ground elder, an umbellifer that flowers after the hedge parsley. The hedges give good cover to robins, wrens, chaffinch and other passerines.

  Keep going to the T-junction with Drumcavel Road at the top of the hill and turn right at the signpost for Muirhead. It is an easy, pleasant walk with good views to the right, but there is traffic on the road and no pavement, so care is needed. Soon the village of Mount Ellen is reached (Mount Ellen Golf Course has been on the left). Take the pavement on the right and just before Gartcosh Motors turn right into an unmarked path with a whitewashed wall on the left, and go uphill. At the top there is a communications mast, with its own approach road alongside the path. There are good views from this point before the path goes downhill to the main Glasgow to Stirling road, a dual carriageway here and busy. Fortunately there are lights not far away in each direction so that traffic tends to pass in batches, making it possible to cross one carriageway at a time. Turn right on the pavement, getting a glimpse of Bedlay Castle through the trees on the left, before reaching the lights to return to the hotel.

Moodiesburn to Gartferry Road

About an hour

From Moodiesburn House Hotel cross Cumbernauld Road by the pedestrian bridge. Prior to crossing the bridge it is interesting to look under the bridge ramps, where there are flower beds that are ignored by the local authority, and which hold a variety of weed species including pineapple weed, with its smell of green apples, common orache, groundsel, knotgrass, sow thistle and mugwort. On the north side of the bridge there are berry-bearing cotoneaster bushes that should be checked for waxwings, thrushes, blackbirds, redwing and fieldfare, depending on the time of year. Turn left into Stoneyetts Road, then left again into Glenmanor Road. Keep on until you reach the foot of the hill and Gartferry Road. Turn left and go on past the roundabout and turn left on to the Railway Walkway. After passing the buildings of the pigeon club on the left, turn right into a footpath known locally as Bow-wow. Follow this to meet Gartferry Road. Turn left up to Chryston Main Street. Turn left, go along past the church and where the road bends to the right keep straight on down the path, with Bedlay Castle on the right. The path bends to the right and under a bridge to reach the main Glasgow to Cumbernauld road (A80). Turn left and go over the pedestrian bridge back to the hotel.

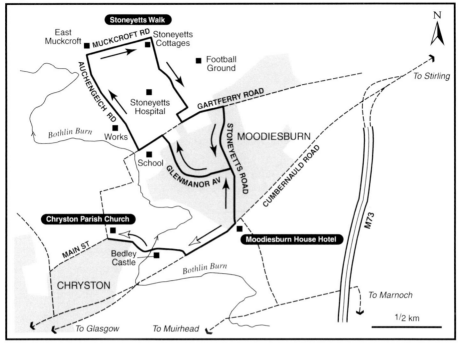

Stoneyetts Hospital

About two hours

From Moodiesburn House Hotel cross Cumbernauld Road by the pedestrian bridge, turn left (north) into Stoneyetts Road, and left again into Glenmanor Avenue and then turn right into Auchengeich Road. Go along to the foot of the hill and turn left into Gartferry Road. On the left-hand side of the road there is a marshy area covered mainly by the smooth rush and other marsh vegetation. A careful examination should find the common spotted orchid. Look at the Memorial on the right commemorating the tragedy at Auchengeich Colliery. At the top of the hill turn right, continue past houses on the right (Stoneyetts Cottages) until you reach the end of a hedge, and turn right down a path. At the end of the path turn right into the former hospital grounds.

To get back to the starting point, go via Glenmuir Crescent, turn right at Gartferry Road into Stoneyetts Road and cross the footbridge. At the time of writing, massive drainage works make the approach to the hospital grounds very muddy, but in the future the grounds may be redeveloped. If it is not possible to explore the grounds, return from Stoneyetts Cottages by the same route.

Moodiesburn to Chryston

About half an hour

From the hotel, cross the main road by the footbridge and turn towards Glasgow. At the end of the houses on the right, opposite Bedlay Cemetery, the road goes over the Walkway and soon there is a track to the right, which is a Right of Way, leading to Bedlay Kennel. Keep on the pavement for another short distance, till you see a sign marked Footpath to Chryston, on the right. Take this, and go under the track, the entrance to which has recently been passed. The path bends to the left and downhill, with Bedlay House towering above on the left. The path goes over the Bothlin Burn and uphill to the first houses of Chryston. The path becomes a road, which is joined by the road leading from the old main road through the village. On the right is the Parish Church, the starting point of the Chryston walks. Return by the same route if not walking in Chryston.

Community history – Don Martin

Chryston

The neighbouring villages of Chryston and Muirhead are laid out in parallel, along Chryston Main Street and the old line of Cumbernauld Road. Chryston is much the older of the two and indeed lies on an even older alignment of the main road, found also at Mount Harriet Drive in Stepps. This was superseded during the 1780s by the turnpike road that now serves as the principal road through Muirhead. One of the toll-houses belonging to this turnpike survives as a dwelling house, on the south side of the road directly opposite the Lindsaybeg Road junction.

The old route at Chryston continues eastwards from Main Street as a path leading down to the site of the old Bedlay well. The gaunt outline of Bedlay Castle towers above this path. The earliest parts of the castle are of mediaeval date and include barrel-vaulted ceilings and a turnpike stair. Families in ownership over the years have included Boyds, Robertsons, Dunlops, Campbells and Christies.

Chryston Main Street is dominated by the Parish Church, opened in 1878 on the site of a former Chapel of Ease. Before the creation of a new *Quad Sacra* Parish of Chryston in the 1870s the parish church was at Cadder. Also in Main Street, and now serving as the parish church hall, is the former Chryston Free Church, dating from the Disruption of the 1840s. The two congregations were reunited in 1929.

Although more recent in origin than Chryston, Muirhead is now the principal centre for shops and related facilities. Development began over 200 years ago, but it was not until cottages and villas were built for Glasgow commuters during the late nineteeenth century that Muirhead grew to any size. The Public Hall was opened, as a "Drill Hall", in 1878 and the Bowling Green in 1900.

Many of the villas and cottages had chimney cans and garden urns made at the famous Garnkirk Fireclay Works close by. The manufacture of fireclay products was a significant local industry during the nineteenth century, with other works at Heathfield and at nearby Cardowan and Gartcosh. Garnkirk Works closed in 1901, but Heathfield continued in business until the 1960s, although only for the manufacture of firebricks and other mundane products. However, it is still possible to find examples of local fireclay vases and urns in the gardens of Muirhead at the present time.

Also at Garnkirk was a station on the first railway to serve the city of Glasgow, the Garnkirk & Glasgow, opened in 1831. The railway is still in use, but the local station was closed to passengers in 1960. Chryston had an even older railway, the Monkland & Kirkintilloch, opened as Scotland's second public railway in 1826. It was at Chryston that the first successful steam locomotive was placed on the rails in 1831. The section of the Monkland & Kirkintilloch serving Chryston closed in 1965.

18

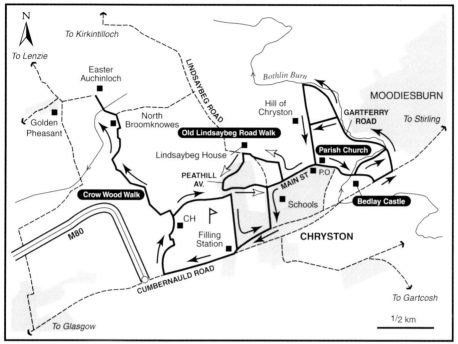

Chryston Parish Church

How to get there. Walk from Moodiesburn, as described. Bus from Kirkintilloch, Coatbridge or Glasgow to Muirhead adjacent to Chryston.

Bedlay Castle

About an hour

From the church, turn left on Main Street and keep straight when the road bends to the right. There are some interesting old houses on the left. The road soon ends. Keep straight on the track downhill to cross the Bothlin Burn, with the imposing Bedlay Castle towering above on the right. *(The walk may be shortened and the stretch along the main road avoided by turning left at this point through a gap in the wall and heading over the hill to join the Walkway where it crosses the Bothlin Burn.)*

    The track goes uphill and bends to the right and under an archway carrying one of the entrances to the house. Until now there has been hardly a sound of traffic, although the track is only a short distance from the A80 Glasgow to Stirling road, one of the busiest in Scotland. Now going under the arch, the roar is loud. Reaching the road, turn left on the pavement and soon, as the coping of the bridge taking the road over the Strathkelvin Railway Walkway is seen, turn left down a small path leading on to the Walkway. Keep on this with a deep gully on the right and a glimpse of the Chryston Church steeple on the left, over the Bothlin Burn which now uses the gully, until a gateway to the Walkway is reached. *(The walk may be extended by staying on the Walkway at this point, crossing the road and continuing on for a short distance. Where the Bothlin Burn goes under, turn left up a path with broken steps alongside a hedge to meet the Gartferry Road at a farm. Follow the road as before up to Main Street and the church.)*

Turn left on to a small track alongside a burn and follow this to Gartferry Road, the road from Bridgend to Chryston. This is part of the Sustrans Cycle Route from Cumbernauld to Glasgow. Cross the road on to the pavement and turn left uphill to Main Street and the church.

Crow Wood

About an hour to the one-way, about two hours round trip

From the church turn right on Main Street, past the post office on the left, the Boys' Brigade and the Church Hall on the right and, on reaching the road from Lenzie, turn left. On the left are the primary and high schools, the Chryston Business Park, the Chilterns Residential Home, the Registry Office of North Lanarkshire Council and the public park. On reaching the Old Cumbernauld Road, turn right through the main shopping centre to the junction with the new road. Keep to the pavement, past the BP filling station and turn right into Crow Wood Golf Club. This is a Right of Way, the use of which is by courtesy of the golf club. The club does not hold itself responsible for any injury sustained and persons using the path do so at their own risk.

Keep on the main drive through a well wooded area, cross the car park, leaving the Club House to the right. Turn right and, keeping the playing area to the right and the woods on the left, join a path leading from one green to the next tee. This has a bridge over the burn. A fence appears on the left and, soon after, a road is reached. This is the entrance to Court Yard Pet Hotel, presumably so called because it is built in the walled garden of Garnkirk House.

Cross the road and soon after cross the Garnkirk Burn. Turn left on the path on the left bank of the burn, entering woods. At the end of these woods, turn right on an almost indiscernible path up to a double line of beech trees. Turn left, alongside the wood that these beech trees have become. Over the field can be seen the former Black and White tower block, now business premises, and in the foreground a substantial white house. At the end of the wood, join the driveway to the house, but turn right, away from the house. The driveway leads to the continuation of Burnbrae Road.

For the one-way trip, return by the same route to the entrance drive to the Pet Hotel, turning left through the golf course to Greenlea Road, following it until it bends left. Going straight on, a short stretch of old road dwindles to a path leading to the BP filling station. Turn left through the village and so back to the church.

Alternatively, turn right on to the extension of Burnbrae Road, follow it and turn left on Burnbrae Road to Auchinloch, Lenzie and Kirkintilloch.

Old Lindsaybeg Road

About half an hour

From the church turn right into Main Street. Before reaching Lindsaybeg Road turn right down the old road. At a corner turn left into a lane, which leads to Lindsaybeg Road. Cross over and go along to a bridge on the left. Cross the bridge into Peathill Avenue. This bends round to the left until a footpath is reached, leading back to Lindsaybeg Road again. Cross over and return by Main Street.

Stepps Walk   Heathfield Moss Walk

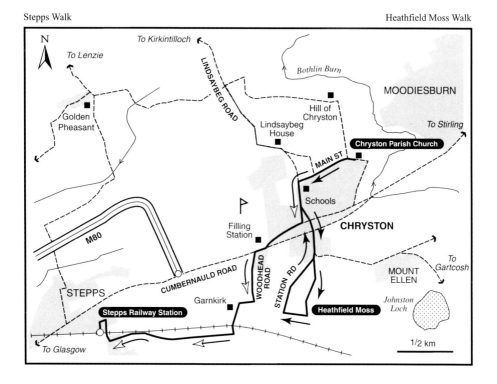

21

Heathfield Moss

About half an hour

From the church turn right then left into Lindsaybeg Road, passing the school on the left and other buildings. Cross diagonally over the park at the lights. Cross the Old Cumbernauld Road and go on down Station Road past the post office to a new roundabout. Cross over and look for a path due south, on the left of the road, to where the station used to be. Follow the path to a junction and turn right (going left would lead to the old station – houses still remain). This leads to Station Road. Turn right back to the roundabout and thence back to the starting point, the church.

Chryston to Stepps

About an hour each way

From the church turn right on Main Street, left at the road from Lenzie and right at the T-junction with Old Cumbernauld Road. Go through the village of Muirhead to the lights, where the old road joins the new road. Cross over and turn right on the footpath. At the first opening, Woodhead Road, opposite the Crow Wood Hotel, turn left and follow the road as it bends through the houses of Garnkirk and out to open fields and over the railway. Now leave Woodhead Road to the right along a path, with the railway line on the right. This leads under a new bridge carrying the road from the huge new roundabout, the start of the M80 to Glasgow. The housing estate on the left is Crow Wood Grange, followed by industrial and commercial development on what was Cardowan Colliery. Keep on the path, with glimpses of the 19th century Gartloch Asylum, now closed, on the left. The view is obscured by the substantial fence surrounding the new houses. Gorse bushes and trees line the path, now called Garnkirk Lane, which now joins Cardowan Road. At the Stewart Inn turn right and cross the railway line. Turn left into Cardowan Drive and left again to Stepps Station.

This walk is known locally as "The Irish Walk", the route taken to reach the only Roman Catholic Chapel in the district.

Community history – Don Martin

Stepps

Stepps is one of several communities in the Glasgow area that can display a detailed and accurate history of its origins. This is because such places were built around their railway station, for settlement by city commuters wishing to live in the country and travel swiftly and cheaply each day to their place of work. Stepps could easily have been the very earliest of these, for it lies on Glasgow's first public railway, the Garnkirk & Glasgow of 1831, and the stopping place there seems to have been the city's first suburban station. However, it was not until the late 1870s that commuters began to arrive in any numbers. They settled at first in Cumbernauld Road, Lenzie Road, West Avenue and Cardowan Drive.

Much of the infrastructure of the original commuter suburb survives. Most of the first houses and shops are still in evidence, as is the Public Hall (opened originally as the "Union Hall", for religious use, in 1885), the Parish Church (opened in Whitehill Avenue in 1900), the School (opened in 1902) and the Bowling Green (opened in 1905). The only major casualties have been the U.F. Church (later St Andrew's) in Blenheim Avenue, which was opened in 1913, closed in 1983 and subsequently demolished; and the original railway station. The station was closed in 1962, but was later replaced by a new one in Cardowan Road, in 1989.

The outstanding feature of nearby Millerston is Hogganfield Loch. During the nineteenth century ice from the loch was popular with Glasgow shops for refrigeratory purposes. At this time, also, the loch began to be used for recreational purposes, especially for skating and curling in winter. During the early years of the twentieth century Glasgow Corporation started to acquire ground at the loch, with a view to creating a public park. A promenade was laid out around the loch and the park formally opened in July 1924. One hundred rowing boats and two motor boats were provided for recreational use. To coincide with the park's opening the Glasgow tramway network was extended from Riddrie to Millerston. The last trams in the area ran in 1959.

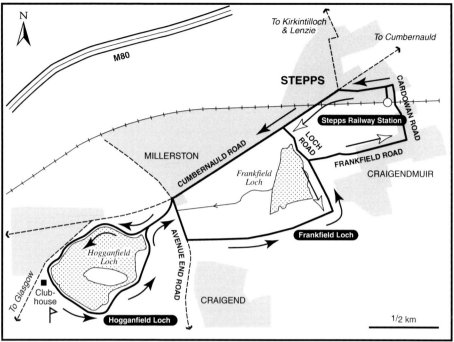

Stepps Railway Station

How to get there. Walk from Chryston, as described. Train from Queen Street, Falkirk Grahamston or Cumbernauld. Through bus Glasgow–Cumbernauld, to junction at Cardowan Drive. Local bus from Kirkintilloch, Lenzie to Cardowan.

Frankfield Loch

About an hour

From the station turn left on Cardowan Drive and left again at the lights at the main Glasgow-to-Stirling road. Turn left (Laundry Lane is on the opposite side of the road). Soon, Frankfield Loch is on the right. This is thought to be the source of the Molendinar Burn, which flows through Hogganfield Loch and in culverts past Glasgow Cathedral to the River Clyde.

The loch area is rich in plant life, including marsh lousewort, bog bean and greater spearwort. On the water great crested grebe, tufted duck, little grebe, coot and the

25

controversial ruddy duck can usually be seen. You should also keep your eyes open for small heath butterflies and toads.

As the track bends to the left, turn right up a small path and through the remnants of an avenue of beech trees, probably the driveway to a large house long since demolished. The corner of the University of Strathclyde Sports Ground, well fenced, is on the right. This is where the walk Clyde Valley Forest turns to the right.

Now return to the path to Cardowan, turn right and you soon reach the houses. Keep on to Cardowan Road. Turn left and so back to the station.

Hogganfield Loch

About two hours

From the station turn left on to Cardowan Drive and left again at the lights on to the main Glasgow-to-Stirling road. Keep going to the lights with the public house on the left. Cross Avenue End Road and enter Hogganfield Loch grounds. The loch was said at one time to be the largest man-made stretch of water within city boundaries in Scotland. The area was favoured by many Glasgow families who brought young children out to what seemed to be the country. It was the terminus of the tram-car route.

Hogganfield Park is one of the City Council's prime sites for biodiversity. At the southeast corner of the loch, several scrapes have been excavated to attract waders and amphibians. In winter the jacksnipe can be found in the area. Wild flowers have been attracted into the adjacent grassland. A family of foxes live in the park and the kestrel is to be seen hovering. An interesting plant to be found at the south end of the loch is the amphibious bistort that thrives in the water and on the land. The main interest on the loch is its bird life. Mute swans can number up to 200 during the summer moult. Goosander – the attractive sawbill duck – can number up to 100 in the winter. Winter is the best time for the birds, when they can be in their thousands and can include such rarities as black-necked grebe, smew and ruddy duck.

The tree-lined tarred path makes a pleasant walk round. Where the path bends to the left, the building is now the clubhouse of Lethamhill Golf Course, also owned and managed by Glasgow City Council. It was at one time the boat house for wintering the dinghies available for hire during the summer. Where the path next bends to the left there is a path to the right, leading out of the grounds and eventually down towards Barlinnie Prison. Returning to the path round the loch, the grassy slopes to the right up the hill may be used to add to the walk, which bends again to the left and so back to the entrance at Avenue End Road. Return to the station by the main road.

An alternative route for the return to the station is by crossing Avenue End Road, turning right and, after the playing fields, left on to a track that is excellent for passerines – robins, wren, chaffinch, blue and great tits and bullfinch – as well as roe deer. The road continues alongside the boundary fence to Frankfield Loch, turning left to the main road and right to Cardowan Drive and the station.

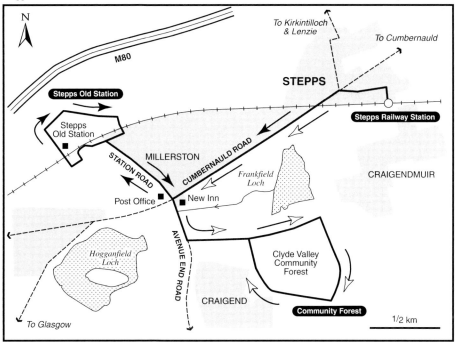

Stepps to Stepps Old Station

About an hour and a half

Leave the station as for the Hogganfield Loch walk. At the entrance to Hogganfield Loch, cross the main Stepps-to-Glasgow road to Station Road and walk on. After the shops, including a well fortified Post Office, there is on the left a new development of flats based on an 18th century tower that has been refurbished after being in ruins for many years. Further over to the left is scrub land, which repays closer inspection. In the damper areas the white-topped cotton grass proliferates, while among the rubbish the attractive northern marsh orchid is found. The area is brightened with the golden meadow vetchling and small heath butterflies.

When the road reaches the end of the houses on the right, it bends to the left, to the footbridge over the Glasgow-to-Falkirk line. Remains of the station can be seen. The rubbish that litters this dump is brightened by clumps of Dame's-violet, which occur in both white and violet colour forms. Common plants that are also to be found are coltsfoot, hedge mustard, meadow buttercup, creeping thistle and shepherd's purse.

Crossing the bridge, the ground is similar scrub and the path is very muddy because of motorbike activity. The track, such as it is, bends to the right and joins an old road. To the left is Junction 1 of the M80 Glasgow to Stirling motorway, and on the hill nearby is more evidence of motorbikes. Now turn right on the old road and follow it to a double bridge, over the Garnkirk Burn and over the railway line. These bridges have been so securely blocked to vehicles that they are almost impassable to walkers, but cross and at the houses turn right and soon Station Road is reached. Turn left and back by the outward route to the new station.

Stepps to Clyde Valley Community Forest

About two hours

Leave the station, and turn left on to Cardowan Drive. At the crossroads turn left, and at the New Inn opposite the entrance to Hogganfiel Loch, walk along Avenue End Road. Pass the frontage of the extensive University of Strathclyde Sports Ground, and turn left on to a broad track. The signboard has a rich cover of graffiti but is just legible as the Clyde Valley Community Forest, now referred to as Cardowan Moss Community Woodland. Walk along the path, with forest on the right and the sports ground on the left, seeing more of the pitches than is possible from the main road. There are several tracks allowing access to the forest, which may be taken as time permits. After a short distance the track bears to the right. Ignoring a smaller track that keeps close to the fence, follow the track down over a strong stone bridge over a burn, and through a marshy area with a fence and a warning notice not to stray from the track. This is Cardowan Moss. The moss contains a raised bog surrounded by wetland habitat where there are skylarks, whinchat, snipe, wheatear, meadow pipit, bullfinch, great and blue tits, wren and reed bunting. The wet areas are good for frogs and toads. Butterflies to be found there are the small heath and the small copper. There is a good selection of plants that include sneezewort, marsh woundwort, soft rush, round-leaved sundew and bottle sedge. In the scrub areas there is goat willow, common spotted and northern marsh orchids. In the grassland areas there is tormentil, sweet vernal grass, meadow buttercup, devil's bit scabious and wild angelica. Rosebay willow herb and thistles invade the grassland. Small rodents and stoat are also found.

Soon the track bears right, with several smaller tracks on the left leading to the houses on the left. There is next a stone-walled exit. At this point either cross diagonally over the grass, to rejoin the forest, or, if it is too wet underfoot, keep to the pavement with the houses on the left. Bear right and through the gap in the houses to a road, with Sunnyside Primary School opposite. Turn right. The road bends to the left and soon meets Avenue End Road. Turn right and so back to the crossroads. Turn right and back to the station.

Cardowan Moss Community Woodland
By Ally Corbett, of KVCP

The land on which Cardowan Community Woodland now stands originally belonged to the now demolished Avenue End Farm but was compulsorily purchased in the 1960s by Glasgow City Council, along with much of the other land in the area, with a view to building housing. Unfortunately for the Council, that particular area of land proved unsuitable, mainly due to subsidence and the presence of a high-pressure gas main.

It remained on the Derelict Land Register until the early 1990s, when Kelvin Valley, in partnership with the newly formed Landwise, a training organisation for the long-term unemployed, undertook the planting of native trees over a six-year period. The aim was to enhance the aesthetic, amenity and wildlife value of the site, acting as a wildlife corridor linking Hogganfield Loch with Frankfield Loch and Bishop Loch, whilst providing training opportunities for local unemployed people. Much of the site is now designated as a Site of Importance for Nature Conservation and has proved very popular with local people.

It is hoped in the near future that the woodland, along with Hogganfield, Bishop Loch and ultimately Drumpellier will form the core area of the "North Glasgow Biodiversity Park" with a continuous footpath network and signage linking all four.

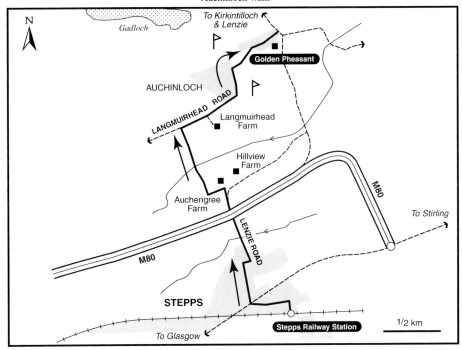

Stepps to Muirhead

About an hour

From the station turn right into Cardowan Drive and left into Cardowan Road. At the main road turn right on the pavement, which is the cycle route from Glasgow to Cumbernauld, and follow it to Muirhead. The Local Authority cut the verges; this tends to remove the more interesting plants. However, when you leave the Buchanan Tower, there are more natural surroundings where the following trees can be identified: oak, lime, ash, rowan, whitebeam, larch, hawthorn, blackthorn and beech. In the verges there is spear thistle, redshank, *Rosa rugosa*, sweet cicely and clumps of brambles. It is here that you may see the whitethroat, singing its scratchy song.

The main street, with shops, cafes and restaurants, is reached by crossing the new main road at the lights to the old road, and turning right. Return by the same route.

Stepps to Auchinloch

About an hour, round trip

From the station turn left into Cardowan Drive and at the lights cross over the main road and along Lenzie Road, passing the tennis courts on the right and the bowling club on the left. The road bends to the right and then to the left, becoming Lenzie Brae. Keep going to the bridge under the motorway, go up the steps on the left along the path under the motorway and up the next steps. At the top turn right and follow the road down to the farm. This is a section of the original road to Lenzie prior to the motorway being built. The hawthorn hedges line the road, giving cover to chaffinches, wrens and tits. Along the verges, especially in summer, a bright golden carpet of meadow buttercups brighten the route. At the farm there is a healthy colony of house sparrows, starlings, crows and gulls. At the farm turn left and go through a gate. After about 100 yards, turn right on to a path with a fence on each side. Cross over two styles and a burn and so on to the Glasgow to Auchinloch road. Turn right (there is no pavement). The road bends to the left at the golf course, then right at the shop and school and up to the village. At the T-junction is the Golden Pheasant, the start of the Auchinloch walks.

Community history – Don Martin

Auchinloch

Until the late nineteenth century Auchinloch was a quiet little country village, fully in tune with the agricultural way of life. Its appearance had not changed much for centuries and thatched cottages could still be seen. There were no pavements and only one short side street. To the north was a notable early example of agricultural improvement. The Loch of Auchinloch had been drained during the early years of the eighteenth century to provide extra agricultural land. A drainage tunnel or "mine" carried the water of the loch into the Park Burn at High Gallowhill and thence to the Kelvin just west of Kirkintilloch. The land gained in this way remained available for agricultural purposes for almost two centuries, but by the end of the nineteenth century the drainage tunnel was blocked and the loch had reappeared on the map. Nowadays the Loch of Auchinloch is usually described as "Lenzie Loch" or "Gadloch". It is regarded as an important amenity on the fringes of Lenzie.

Industrialisation came to Auchinloch in the early 1880s, when the nearby Lumloch Colliery was opened up by the Carron Company. In succeeding years various problems were experienced at the pit and it closed down during the very early 1900s. During the 1920s, however, the derelict workings were purchased by James Nimmo & Co. and reopened as 'Wester Auchengeich Colliery'. Soon afterwards Nimmo & Co. built 153 cottage-type houses for the Wester Auchengeich miners at Western Auchinloch (First–Fourth Avenues) – a significant milestone in Auchinloch history. Electric power for Western Auchengeich Colliery was supplied from a plant at neighbouring Auchengeich Colliery (Chryston), where there were problems following a major disaster in 1959. Wester Auchengeich finally closed in 1968.

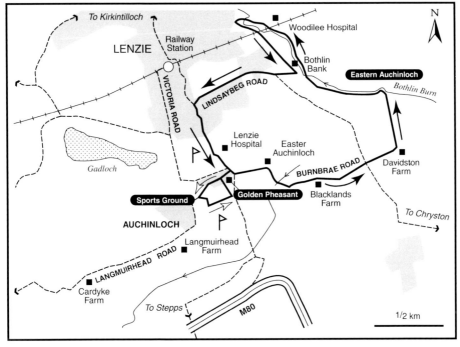

Auchinloch Golden Pheasant

How to get there. Walk from Stepps, as described. Bus Glasgow–Kirkintilloch.
Local bus Kirkintilloch–Cardowan.

Auchinloch Sports Ground

About half an hour

Leave the Golden Pheasant by the back and turn left into Langmuirhead Road. The
architecture of the houses on each side spans many years and illustrates quite different
styles. The former school is now the Community Centre. The grassy area on the right is
a blaze of yellow when the daffodils are in bloom. Where the road is flanked on both
sides by the golf course, turn left on to a broad track leading to the Auchinloch Playing
Fields, a mini-football pitch and a play area for young children. Go past the pavilion,
alongside a fence; cross a stile and turn left. On the right-hand side of the path at the start
of the Right of Way, there is a marshy area where the smooth rush grows profusely. This
is an area that usually holds water but can dry out in summer time. Mallard ducks, wagtails

and waders may to seen here. In the open area, the skylark still sings, while in the hedgerows wrens, robins and dunnock are active.

This Right of Way leads up to Langmuirhead Road. Turn right to go back to the Golden Pheasant.

Easter Auchinloch

About an hour

From the Golden Pheasant cross the Lenzie-to-Stepps road and go along Burnbrae Road. The first house on the left was the local police station. As the road bends to the left, note the house on the right, originally a weaver's cottage. At the top of the hill is Blacklands Farm. A bungalow is on the left, before the crossroads. On the left can be seen the Millersneuk marsh, which gives excellent birdwatching, with species such as garganey duck turning up. Go straight over, passing the deserted Davidson Farm. The road bends left. At the top of the hill, dogs in the grounds of the house will make their presence known. On the right is Burnbrae Farm, whose owner has recently created a woodland open to the public. Access is at the foot of the hill, on the right. If not visiting the wood, turn left on to the Railway Walkway along the Bothlin Burn. As you walk along the Bothlin Burn, look out for water voles. This used to be an excellent area for them until a few years ago, when they were sadly reduced by mink and youths with airguns. There are several schemes being promoted by local authorities to bring back the water vole, and there are successes in the area, so hopefully they will return. Perhaps you will be the first to report the successful return!

Keep on the Walkway, passing a marshy area on the right, to a crossing near a house. Turn right over a wooden bridge. On the right is a weir, made to take water along a lade to the Forth and Clyde Canal at South Bank, Kirkintilloch, which has good-quality water and in which you will find duckweed and Canadian pondweed growing. KVCP recently looked into the feasibility of installing a fish pass on the weir to allow fish further up the Bothlin Burn to spawn. Unfortunately, local anglers were of the opinion that upstream was still too polluted to be suitable, and the scheme has been shelved for the meantime.

Take the path to the left, following the lade under the railway bridge (a problem for the engineers designing the Kirkintilloch relief road). The path ends inside the entrance to Woodilee Hospital. Turn left on to the road leading to Garngaber Avenue, left again on to the Walkway, and return to the Golden Pheasant.

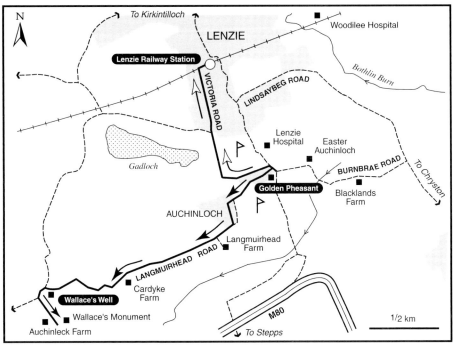

Wallace's Well and Monument

About two hours

From the Golden Pheasant turn left on to Langmuirhead Road past the school, leaving the general store on your left, unless you wish to provide yourself with some sustenance. At the bowling club turn left into First Avenue, which leads you down to rejoin Langmuirhead Road, where you turn right. The pavement stops at the end of the village so care is needed. Perhaps the Local Authority will construct a footpath to this important monument. At the roadside can be seen ash and sycamore trees. On the left-hand side is also a new plantation of trees, and by the roadside there are patches of stinging nettle, which are a good source of butterflies – small tortoiseshell and red admiral. On the fields on the right, geese from the Gadloch can be seen grazing in the winter months.

　　　Langmuirhead Farm is on the left. The next building on the left is a cats' protection Cardyke Farm Shelter. Follow the road until it meets the road from Lenzie to Robroyston. You have just crossed the boundary into Glasgow District and are at Wallace's Well. The burn flowing past and under the road goes on into Gadloch. Its source appears to be a spring on the north side of Robroyston Hill. The name is often thought to be derived from

35

Rob Roy's Town. Continuing on the road past Auchenleck Farm, you arrive at Wallace's Monument, well preserved in a gravelled, fenced plot, with several inscriptions clearly legible. Return by the same route.

Auchinloch to Lenzie

Less than an hour

Leave the Golden Pheasant and turn left on Langmuirhead Road; go through the village until the road is flanked by the golf course. At the school, turn right on a path that leaves the school on the left and the golf course on the right and goes downhill with the Gadloch on the left. The footpath is liable to flooding when the Gadloch backs up. In the OS map of 1897 there is no sign of a loch at this location, but owing to mine washings and the partial blocking of the culvert that drains the area the loch was formed. The local angling club no doubt encouraged the partial blocking of the outlet to increase the fishing area. The Gadloch, owing principally to the large overwintering flock of greylag geese, is considered to be a priority water by the Wildfowl Trust. In the winter there are large numbers of duck and waders, but summer breeding numbers of birds are disappointing, mainly because of disturbance caused by fishermen. There is also a threat due to the ongoing housing developments that are marching towards the Gadloch.

On the right-hand side of the path there is a marshy area where the smooth rush grows profusely. This is an area that usually holds water but can dry out in summertime. Mallard duck, wagtails and waders may be seen here. In the open area the skylark still sings, while in the hedgerows wrens, robins and dunnock are active. On a clear day there is a splendid view of the Campsies and the hills west of Loch Lomond. The loch frequently floods over the path and the golf course; a detour to the right is then required. Cross the main road and go up Victoria Road, turn right at the T-junction and left into the station, the starting point of the Lenzie walks.

Community history – Don Martin

Lenzie

The name "Lenzie" is very old indeed, although the same cannot be said of the place that now bears it. The original Lenzie was an ecclesiastical parish that extended from Kirkintilloch north-westwards as far as Cumbernauld. The lands of Lenzie were for many years possessed in their entirety by the Comyn family, who built a castle at Kirkintilloch. The name was pronounced "Lingie" at that time, and for many years thereafter.

The history of modern Lenzie can be traced back only to the year 1842, when the Edinburgh & Glasgow Railway was opened and a station established there to serve the town of Kirkintilloch. The building of houses for Glasgow commuters, close to the station, began about 1848 and was given impetus by the railway company's scheme of the 1850s to offer free season tickets to persons building large villas near any of its stations. However, large-scale construction did not begin until piped running water was made available to the villas during the 1870s, by which time the free "villa tickets" scheme had been discontinued. The housing and population boom of the 1870s is reflected in the fact that all three of Lenzie's main churches – the Old Parish, the Union Parish and St Cyprian's – were established during that decade. The growth of Lenzie, as a convenient place of residence for Glasgow commuters, has continued ever since.

The railway station was opened to serve the town of Kirkintilloch and was accordingly named "Kirkintilloch" at first. During the 1840s it was relocated to Garngaber for a short period. In 1848 it was moved back to its present site, and with the opening of a branch line to Lennoxtown it was renamed "Campsie Junction". The extension of this branch to Campsie Glen and beyond, in 1867, gave rise to an anomaly over the station name, and the railway company (by then the North British) chose the old parochial name of "Lenzie" to replace it. The station and its environs have been known as Lenzie ever since (although pronounced differently from the old parish name).

When in Lenzie, the castellated villa known as "The Tower", at the corner of Kirkintilloch Road and Garngaber Avenue, should be noted. Built in 1858, this was one of the houses to benefit from the Edinburgh & Glasgow Railway's free season tickets scheme. The Old Parish Church, just across the road, is one of the churches of the 1870s, mentioned above. A short distance downhill, towards Kirkintilloch, is the Union Church, where several stained glass windows in memory of notable early commuters can be seen.

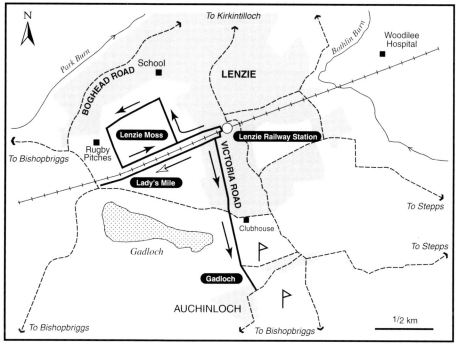

Lenzie Railway Station

How to get there. Walk from Auchinloch, as described. Bus Glasgow–Kirkintilloch. Local bus Kirkintilloch–Cardowan.

Lenzie–Gadloch

About half an hour

Leave the station by the booking office side, turn right along the path to Alexandra Avenue and then left into Victoria Road. This is one of several Conservation Areas in Lenzie in which there are restrictions as to what changes may be made to property – permission even having to be obtained to lop or fell trees. Some new houses were built after the original ones of distinctive 1870 vintage. The only open spaces are the Jubilee Gardens at the corner of Heriot Road, the entrance to the "Royal" estate (Anne Crescent, Andrew Avenue and Charles Crescent) and the segment made when Crosshill Road was straightened. Cross this road and follow the footpath between the golf course practice ground and MacLaren's Farm. This is a Right of Way. The path is liable to flooding when the Gadloch backs up.

39

On the OS map of 1897 there is no sign of a loch in this location. It had been drained by a remarkable initiative on the part of William Marshall, a Glasgow merchant who had acquired the rights to land at the loch from local proprietors, thereby originating a scheme to drive a drainage tunnel from the north-west corner of the loch to the Park Burn. This enabled land that had formerly been under water to be used for farming purposes. Some of the vertical shafts that had been constructed at intervals along the tunnel may still be seen. Eventually the tunnel became blocked and the loch "came back". The Gadloch, principally because of the large over-wintering by flocks of Greylag geese, is considered by the Wildfowl Trust to be a priority water. Also in the winter there are large numbers of ducks and waders. In the summer, numbers of breeding birds are disappointing, perhaps on account of disturbance caused by fishing.

Return by the same route.

Lady's Mile
About half an hour

Leave the station by the booking office side, turning right along Station Lane. At the end are two strange containers which turn out, on enquiry, to be lockable bicycle sheds for the use of commuters. On the left is an unusually designed building that has had several different uses in its time, from grocer shop to solicitor's cum building society representative's. Turn into Alexandra Avenue. The shops under the flats have also had many owners and tenants. At one time, when there was prohibition north of the railway line, the licensed grocer was in demand. This is now a doctor's surgery, part time. The library has a remarkably large stock, considering its small size, and the staff are extremely helpful in borrowing books from other branches. At the corner of Alexandra Avenue and Alexandra Road is the start of the narrow footpath owned and maintained by the railway authorities. It was originally created for passengers from Boghead Road to gain access to the station and is now a Right of Way, much used by dog-walkers. The ground on the left is also owned by the railway authorities, and is part of Lenzie Moss.

You can look to your right over the railway into the Lenzie Moss area, where birch trees are causing the moss to dry out. Over the moss you may see the resident kestrel hunting. Nearing the road bridge there is a wet area on the left-hand side which supports a variety of weed species including the stinging nettle, which can be used to make soup, a vegetable dish and a pudding, which can be washed down with nettle wine or nettle beer. Ground elder is also there. This was probably introduced by the Romans, and was used extensively as a vegetable. Continue on the path as far as Crosshill Road, then retrace your steps to the station.

Lenzie Moss
About an hour

Leave the station from the side opposite the booking office and turn left through the station car park, entering the wooded part of the Moss. Take the first path on the right, which has been made up by prisoners from Low Moss Prison, arranged by The Friends of Lenzie Moss. This crosses diagonally, leaving the houses and several of the avenues, leading to the main road on the right. On the left is the main area which was at one time worked commercially for peat. The Council are hoping to achieve a compulsory purchase of this area of land, so that the Moss may be designated and managed as a local nature reserve. The ground on the right is owned by the Lenzie Rugby club, with several pitches in use and further development in evidence. Further on the right is Lenzie Moss Primary School. The path bends to the left with the backs of a row of houses on the right. At any point from there on, a route can be found through the trees to a hill of peat, from where a good view can be obtained. This part of the walk is boggy, and gumboots are needed. Keep on in a southerly direction until you reach the main railway line, and turn left along the path through the wood, back to the station.

Lenzie Moss: local nature reserve
By Jackie Gillespie, of KVCP

Most people would never expect to find a 10,000-year-old peat bog right on the doorstep of one of Glasgow city's urban satellites. However, Lenzie Moss – comprising 47 square hectares of remnant peat bog, wet birch woodland and unimproved grassland – provides habitat for a wide range of plants and animals and can be found right on the edge of Lenzie itself.

The peat bog itself is extremely wet; in fact an undamaged peat bog consists of 90% water and only 10% organic matter. Some plants have adapted to these conditions. The Sundew can be found throughout the peat bog areas of Lenzie Moss, where it supplements its nutrient intake by trapping midges on its sticky leaves and then slowly digests them.

Lenzie Moss is also noted for the presence of Bog Rosemary, a small shrubby plant related to blaeberry. Bog Rosemary, with its delicate pale pink bell-shaped flowers, is now a nationally rare species, owing to habitat destruction; at Lenzie Moss, it is found only on the uncut peat bog area.

It is known that Lenzie Moss has been cut for peat since 1226, when the Canons of Cambuskenneth were granted a charter allowing this. Subsequent drainage of the centuries, disturbance by the building of the Glasgow–Edinburgh railway, commercial peat cutting and wilful fire raising has changed its nature from the immense "Mountain Moss" to a network of baulks and peat fields with a small periphery of uncut peat bog on its western edge.

Birch trees have invaded the "Moss", drying the bog further and changing it in places to wet birch woodland. Secretive Woodcock hide in these woodlands, usually only becoming active at night. In spring, however, the males can be seen displaying at dusk, when they fly low in a straight line and call with a wheezy croak. Long-tailed tits, great tits, blue tits and chaffinches also feed and breed in these areas, and are in turn prey to the sparrow hawk, a top predator in these woodlands.

To the north of Lenzie Moss, overlooking the cut peat fields, large areas of blaeberry can be found. Sheltered by nearby open birch woodland, they provide a sunny, still environment for the Green Hairstreak Butterfly, Britain's only green butterfly. For about three weeks in May, this small species flies on sunny still days, when it is well worth spending some time looking for this most attractive butterfly.

Other attractive insects abound on the "Moss". The Common Hawker Dragonfly can be seen from June until the first autumn frosts. Belonging to an ancient group of insects, it is also one of the fastest of insects, catching its prey on the wing, even flying backwards to do so. The smaller damselflies can be seen from May onwards. Species such as the Large Red Damselfly are common along the peat baulks, where they feed on midges. Observant walkers may notice pale or "ghost" damselflies. These are Tenerals, newly emerged damselflies that have not yet developed their colouring.

Lenzie Moss is criss-crossed with a network of desire-line paths, where walkers have created their own specific circuits around the "Moss". There is also an important Right of Way from the railway station to Blackthorn Avenue, which is heavily used by school children, cyclists and dog walkers. It is planned that parts of Lenzie Moss will be bought by East Dunbartonshire Council, with the view to creating a local nature reserve. A management plan has been drawn up with the view of rehabilitating the peat bog, improving the woodlands and creating a safe network of paths for the area. Lenzie Moss, with its diverse range of plants and animals, has managed to survive for 10,000 years; can it be possible to help it survive for 10,000 more?

There is a Lenzie Moss Education Pack compiled and published by KVCP. A copy is available in each local school.

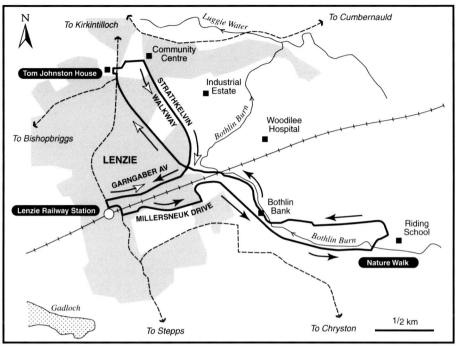

Lenzie nature walk

About an hour

Come out of the car park on the north side of the station. Turn right and walk down Auchinloch Road, under the railway bridge, and take the first left into Millersneuk Road. The shopping development is on the right and the walk now passes through a small plantation of mature beech, elm, sycamore, ash and plane. One of the elm trees is diseased – possibly owing to Dutch elm disease, which is caused by a fungus transmitted by elm bark beetles. This is an area where grey squirrels are sometimes seen.

On the right-hand side of the road is the Cult Burn, which gives its name to Cult Road. The burn is difficult to access at this point, because of fencing and hedging. Before coming to the first house on the left-hand side of the road, you will find an area that can be good for seeing blue and great tits. In winter, redwing and fieldfare have been seen here. Continue along Millersneuk Drive, alongside the Cult Burn, and turn left at Eastergarngaber Road. Continue past the road bollards on the left-hand side of the road, and turn up a track on the right-hand side, immediately before the railway bridge.

43

The area on the left-hand side of the track has been used over the years to dump garden rubbish; look out for garden escapees such as yellow loosestrife and lungwort. The sides of the track should also be inspected for ground ivy and pink purslane. Pink purslane can have either pink or white flowers, so do not be misled by the white-flowering form.

At the top of the track the walker finds himself alongside the main Glasgow–Edinburgh line, and, although the path is fenced, care should be taken if small children or dogs are in the party. Houses were constructed on the right-hand side of the old colliery railway line in 1958. The railway line was constructed on slag ballast, which tends to be basic and well drained, with slightly different flower and insect communities from adjoining areas. The old railway line now diverges from the main line, with the area between the lines being taken over mainly by birch and willow scrub.

This is an open area, where it is worth looking for birch-related fungi. In the late summer or autumn the well known fly agarics (*Amanita muscaria*) should be seen. This is red with white spots, and is to be seen in illustrations of many fairy-tales. Puffballs may also be found here. Unless you are an expert micologist do not try eating toadstools or mushrooms.

The old railway line, which linked Lenzie with Auchingeich many years ago, now leaves the housing development on the right-hand side, where mature privet and snowberry occur. Both shrubs provide berries, which are good feeding for birds. Another shrub to be seen at this location is bride's blossom.

At this point the Cult Burn runs under the embankment in a brick culvert to discharge into the Bothlin Burn, which now runs on your left-hand side parallel to the line of the old railway. Bats sometimes use culverts for winter hibernation.

Good views can now be had of the adjoining countryside. Magpies, crows, wood pigeon and rooks are usually to be seen, and the yellowhammer is often seen on the telephone wires that run along the railway line. In the autumn, this part of the walk is excellent for gathering brambles and rosehips. The following flowers are a few of those that can be seen: yarrow, sneezewort, redleg, knapweed, pineappleweed, birds' foot trefoil, meadow vetchling and eyebright.

Continue along the line until you see a cottage on the left-hand side, and you will find yourself at a crossroads. Keep on the track alongside the burn until a road is reached. Turn left and uphill, passing a riding school. At the next junction turn left. The road bends left. When it bends to the right, go through the gate there.

At this point the route is fairly high and good views are obtained. You are walking alongside a farmer's fields and due respect should be shown to the farmer's property. Follow an old track down the hill to the bridge over the Bothlin Burn at the cottage. Approaching the bridge, keep a lookout for redwing, fieldfare and brambling, which tend to feed and shelter in the hawthorn thickets on the left-hand side in the winter. This is also a good location for sparrowhawk and kestrel.

Pause at the timber bridge over the burn. Immediately upstream is a weir, which enables water to be drawn off to feed the Forth and Clyde Canal. The walk now continues towards Woodilee Hospital, with the Bothlin Burn on the left and the canal feeder on the right. This is a good place to look for river birds. On a lucky day you may see dipper, grey wagtail, kingfisher and heron; coal, blue and great tits may also be seen.

The walk now passes a mature stand of Scots Pine. Unfortunately, owing to people pressure, there is no regeneration. In a Scottish Wildlife Trust reserve, cones would be gathered and the seeds planted. The resulting seedlings would be planted out in plastic tubes to protect the trees at their vulnerable stage. There are normally coal tits in the pines, and you might be fortunate to see a crossbill. Fungi tend to relate to particular plants or trees. In the pinewood in autumn the false chanterelle is said in some books to be edible but in others is said to cause alarming symptoms.

The route passes through mature woodland until the main drive to the hospital is reached. Turn left and join Garngaber Road back to the station.

Railway Walkway to Tom Johnston House

About an hour

Leave the station by the exit opposite the booking office, cross the car park, turn left past the shops and cross with the green man into Garngaber Avenue. The church on the right is Lenzie Old Parish Church. The third house on the left is Abbeyfield Home. Passing Lomond Road on the left, Easter Garngaber Road on the right and Garngaber Court on the left, turn left onto the Railway Walkway. After a quarter of a mile or so, the path divides about 100 yards before its exit to Middlemuir Road. Along this section of the walkway can be seen ground elder, convolvulus, yellow archangel, and lords and ladies –the attractive arum. Take the left fork and the end of this branch is reached at White Gates, called after the level crossing, the gates being in existence long after the line was dismantled.

Cross the main road at the pedestrian lights to Tom Johnston House, the headquarters of East Dunbartonshire Council. During office hours the staff restaurant on the top floor is open to the public. Across the park is the site of the former swimming baths, demolished in 1999, and greatly missed. The remaining building is the community centre. To the left is the more formal part of the park with well tended flowerbeds and shrubs. The display of daffodils on the road verge is splendid in season. After leaving Tom Johnston House, cross the main road again at the pedestrian lights and cross the grass diagonally to the corner, where there are swings for youngsters. At the fence enclosing the cutting of the former railway line from Glasgow to Aberfoyle, turn right behind the community centre to the other fork of the Walkway. This is a protected area with undergrowth left uncut to provide a suitable habitat for wildlife. Willow, birch, rowan, hawthorn and elder trees fight it out with brambles and nettles, which safeguard the local insect life from disturbance. Other plants to look out for are colt's foot and rosebay willowherb, which covered the bomb sites in London at the end of the last war.

On the left is a football pitch and on the right between the two forks of the Walkway is an open grassy space for games, with an area for small children. In winter the grassed areas are good for seeing flocks of winter thrushes – redwing and fieldfare. At the junction with Garngaber Road turn right to reach the main road and the station.

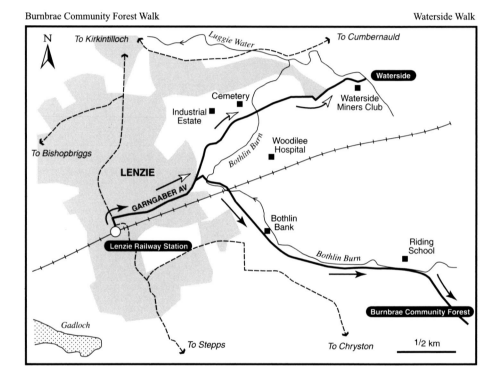

Walkway to Burnbrae Community Forest

About an hour and a half

Leave the station by the exit opposite the booking office, cross the car park, turn left past the shops, cross the main road at the lights and go along Garngaber Avenue past Easter Garngaber Road and turn right onto the Railway Walkway. On the right is a row of Victorian villas, known locally as The Seven Sisters. On the left is a feeder for the Forth and Clyde Canal. The next point of interest is the bridge carrying the Glasgow to Edinburgh and Stirling railway line. When walking under the bridge on a summer's evening you may see bats issuing from a hole in the underside of the bridge. The bats are probably Pipistrelles. Just past this the Bothlin Burn is joined by the Cult Burn, which flows under the path. After a quarter of a mile or so, there is a house on the left; another footpath from Lenzie merges and there are two gates, one on each side of the roadway that gives access to the house and to a bridge over the Bothlin Burn. From the bridge there is a good view of the weir that is the feeder for the canal. Continue along the Walkway. Look out for Mallard, Teal and Moorhen. If you are lucky, you may see a Kingfisher flashing up or down the burn. The next stone gateways allow you to cross the road from Auchinloch to Kirkintilloch. This is the start of Burnbrae Wood on the right of the Walkway to begin with, and then on both sides. The grass is kept short to form footpaths, and there are benches. After spending some time exploring, return along the Walkway as far as the house near the weir. Do not take the immediate left path but the one between it and the Walkway. This leads up towards the main-line railway and then turns down to Garngaber Road. Turn right under the railway bridge and then left into Garngaber Avenue and back to the station.

Lenzie to Waterside

About two hours round trip

Leave the station by the exit opposite the booking office, cross the car park, turn left past the shops, cross the main road at the lights and go along Garngaber Avenue. Where this takes an S-bend at the entrance to Woodilee Hospital, with a glimpse of the Bothlin Burn, leave the road and cross over the field, taking the right fork at the top of the incline towards a row of houses signed Woodilee Cottages, formerly staff quarters of the hospital. The field used to contain horses, but in 2000 it was lying fallow and gave a great show of wild flowers – meadow buttercup, creeping buttercup, ox-eye daisy, ragwort, lady's mantle, common spotted orchid – and trees such as elm, ash, hawthorn and alder. Have a good look at this hay meadow because at least part will disappear when the proposed development of Woodilee Hospital grounds takes place and the Kirkintilloch Relief Road is constructed – if ever!

Turn right, cross the road and turn left between the houses. After passing at the back of industrial buildings, there is a view of the Auld Aisle Cemetery and an opportunity to browse among the gravestones if desired. The path at this point used to go over the stream by the Spider Bridge, so called because of its apparently fragile construction and height above the water – or because it had eight legs. A sturdy low-level wooden bridge has replaced it, but this means a steep climb up to the boundary wall of Woodilee Hospital grounds. Turn right then left after the bridge to use the steps, avoiding an even steeper shortcut. A pause here gives time to view the Campsie Fells. The path leads on to Calfmuir Road. Turn left, and pass Duntiblae Road coming in from the left. At the crossroads go straight over and into Duntiblae village. Confusingly, the most prominent building is the Waterside Miners' Welfare Social Club, and further on is the Duntiblae village shop. At the footbridge over the Luggie Water is Waterside. Either turn and go back to Lenzie, or take the opportunity to explore some of the walks described for Waterside.

As an alternative return route, cross the footbridge and turn left, and after 200–300 yards turn left again onto the signposted footpath to Bridgend. At the end of this path turn left along Waterside Road at the traffic lights and, after a very short distance, take the first left off the main road and the first right on to what will later be signposted as Bridgeway Road, which veers round to the right exit off and into Bridgeway Terrace. At the T-junction with Old Aisle Road turn left up to and through the cemetery gates. Follow the main path round to the grassed roundabout, after which take the first left and go downhill and through the gates, turning right onto the path that will lead you past Woodilee Cottages. So retrace your steps back to Lenzie railway station.

Community history – Don Martin

Waterside

In former times Waterside was famed for its neat and tidy weavers' cottages on the north bank of the Luggie, some slated and some thatched, and its picturesque mills on the south bank. In between lay a well-built mill dam, which overflowed as an attractive waterfall, between river levels. During the 1890s the whole scene was described as "uncommonly beautiful".

Many of the former weavers' cottages survive but the mills have long since been demolished. The mill dam has collapsed into a random scattering of stones on the river bed. The upper of the two mills was situated beside the dam, and was a justifiably popular subject for picture postcards. It was built in 1779, as a lint mill for the processing of flax for the local linen industry. Further downstream was the Earl of Wigton's ancient corn mill of Duntiblae, where local people from a wide area round about were obliged to take their grain for grinding. A lade, or water course, led from the mill dam first to the lint mill, then several hundred yards downstream to the corn mill, to supply both with water. Remains of the lade channel can still be discerned on the south bank of the Luggie, near the footbridge.

The corn mill was burned down during the middle years of the nineteenth century but was rebuilt as a factory for making spades and shovels. The lint mill was later adapted as an auxiliary of the shovel works.

Another interesting building at Waterside is the former Subscription School, which survives just north of the footbridge. An inscription provides the information that it was erected in 1839 by Wm. Aitken & Co., contractors. The Subscription School was superseded by Gartconner School and later served as a meeting place for a variety of local organisations.

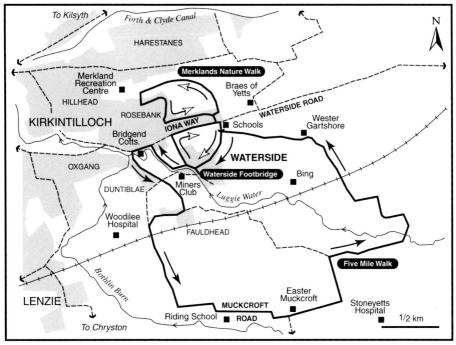

Waterside

How to get there. Walk from Lenzie, as described. Bus Kirkintilloch–Twechar. The Waterside walks start and finish at the footbridge over the river Luggie at Bankhead Road, Waterside.

The Five Mile Walk

About two and a half hours

The Five Mile Walk, as it is known locally, is actually 5.2 miles long and is mostly along pleasant but narrow country roads without footpaths. For safety, walk facing the oncoming traffic, although there are exceptions to this, e.g. approaching a sharp right-hand bend, when it is safer to cross to the other side.

    Starting at the footbridge, cross Bankhead Road on the pavement side and walk in the direction of Kirkintilloch for about 150 metres, then cross the road to the signpost showing "Footpath to Bridgend". This section is a short but attractive path where heron, dipper and grey wagtail can be seen. On reaching the top of the steps at the end of this section, turn left, along Waterside Road. About 200 metres along, you come to Bridgend Cottages, where you turn left into Market Road (road sign points to Fauldhead). At the top of the hill is a crossroads. You now leave the houses behind and the country lane is bounded by overgrown hedges that have bramble, elm and birch growing in them. The hedges are excellent for dunnocks, chaffinches and blue tits.

Go straight ahead on a narrow road to a row of red brick houses and a large water tower; this is Fauldhead. Turn right into Blairhill Avenue and, just past the water tower, the landscape opens out and there are chestnut, lime and sycamore trees. In the autumn the sycamore leaves have black spots. This is the tar fungus that helps to break down the leaves and recycle them. There is also a large patch of nettles, which is good for red admiral and small tortoiseshell butterflies. The road at this point seems unnecessarily wide, but this was the site of the large home farm that served Woodilee Hospital. At the fork in the road bear left, and at the main road turn left. As you cross the bridge over the Glasgow–Edinburgh railway line, note the ornamental field gate on the left. At the top of the hill pause to enjoy the views.

After a series of bends, the road comes to a T-junction at Strathkelvin Riding Centre. Bear left along the road, which has a crash barrier. On reaching the stone walls of an old railway bridge, the Meikle Bin can be seen just above the Campsies. The fields on the left are good for large flocks of birds – especially in the winter, when starlings and rooks feed on invertebrates and flocks of geese can be seen grazing. The route goes past two sharp bends and straight on uphill, passing East Muckcroft Farm on the left, where there are further good views of the Campsie and Kilsyth hills. At a single row of houses, the road turns left and downhill; at the next T-junction turn right. Very soon the road crosses the River Luggie via an old arched stone bridge. Take time to view the bridge from the river bank.

About 150 yards from the bridge, the road forks. Bear left and eventually you pass under the Glasgow–Edinburgh railway line. Just before Wester Gartshore, on the left, is a small dilapidated cemetery under a clump of trees. This is a Quaker family cemetery; the date on one gravestone is 1780. The route now passes the lodge and gates to Gartshore Estate, one-time home of Lord William Whitelaw. Along the road and 100 yards past Gartconner Primary School, where the road bends, cross Berryknowe and Back O' Dykes Road, to Bankhead Road, where the walk started.

Merklands Nature Park

About one and a half hours, depending on the level of interest in wildlife

Starting from the footbridge over the Luggie, cross Bankhead Road to the pavement side. The first building has an interesting plaque on the wall: "Waterside Subscription School May 24 1839". Further along, a house is called "The Hoolets", another "Weavers Sheiling" and then more prosaically "Waterside Cottages". Continue on to the junction with the main road from Kirkintilloch, Waterside Road, and turn right. After a short distance, when a road sign for Wester Gartshore can be seen, and St Agatha's and Gartconner primary schools are passed, cross the road and go down Iona Way. At the pillar-box turn right into Bute Road, which ends after a few metres. Turn left in to a footpath leading to Merklands Nature Park. The field on the right is waterlogged; the farm at the far side of the field is Braes of Yetts. On the left is the park with scrubby trees and plants, as would be expected in such conditions.

The path continues over a couple of footbridges over small streams, and bends left. Keep to the left fork, as taking the right one would lead out of the park. The same would appear to be the case at the next fork, but take the right one and as soon as the football pitch is reached bear left, over a wooden bridge, and then right. The path now broadens out and in the distance can to seen the tall lights of the Merklands Outdoor Recreation Centre. When the path meets Merklands Drive, turn left for a few metres and then left again, back into the park. Keep going past a place that appears to have been a bing, now more or less flattened, but still affording a viewpoint. After a short distance there is a prominent grassy area on the left. At the end of this, the path turns right and meets Iona Way. Turn left, and at the pillar-box the road bends to the right to meet Waterside Road. Cross over and turn right, and soon leave the pavement by a track leading round the football pitch. Going along the road between houses, pass a roundabout and join Bankhead Road. Turn left and back to the footbridge.

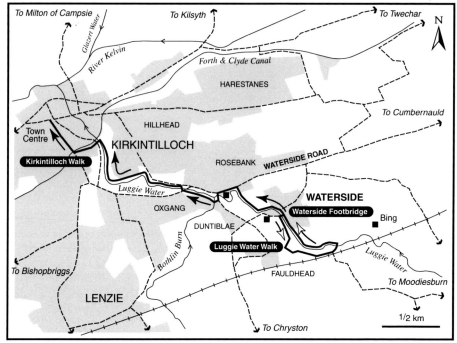

Luggie Water

About three-quarters of an hour

Starting from Bankhead Road, go onto the footbridge, from where you can see willows and alders on the riverbanks. These are trees that enjoy wet areas, especially the alder, which can transfix atmospheric nitrogen using nodules in its root system. Beside the footbridge there is a stand of comfrey, which is a medicinal herb, known to the Crusaders as a herb for wounds, repairing broken bones and battered bodies. Cross the footbridge and turn sharp left, following the path through a kissing gate at the top of the hill. Fauldhead is on the right. From here there are good views towards Kirkintilloch.

Once through the gate, turn left onto a minor road (Chryston Road). Further along, the road runs parallel and close to the Glasgow–Edinburgh railway line. It then turns sharp right and under the railway. Just at the bend, BEFORE going under the railway, cross the road to an opening marked by two "No Dumping" signs, where a narrow but well defined footpath can be seen. This path soon leads to a bridge over the Luggie, which originally carried vehicles serving Waterside Pit, but is now for pedestrians only. On crossing the bridge the path splits in three different directions. Turn left and follow the path along the riverbank.

As you make your way along this very pleasant stretch of the Luggie, look out for the large stepping-stones that are part of a Right of Way used by the miners of Waterside, walking to and from the Auchengeich Pit. A few hundred yards further along, the path ends back at the footbridge in Waterside.

Waterside to Kirkintilloch

Round trip about an hour and a half

Start at the footbridge and walk along Bankhead Road in the direction of Kirkintilloch for about 150 yards, then cross the road to the signpost showing "Footpath to Bridgend". Walk along this pleasant riverside path where there are ash, birch and sycamore trees as well as laurel bushes. Entomologists used the laurel leaves in the past to kill insects. The insect was put in a jar with the crushed leaves, which released acid fumes.

On reaching the top of the steps at the end of this section, turn left, along Waterside Road. About 200 yards along, you come to Bridgend Cottages, where you turn left into Market Road. Cross over to the red pillar-box. A few yards beyond the pillar-box, cross the footbridge over the Bothlin Burn where it joins the Luggie. Beside the bridge you will see cotoneaster bushes which in the autumn bear a berry harvest, which may give you the opportunity to see winter visiting waxwings, which come across from the Continent to harvest our berry crop. At the riverside there are crack willow, ash and the red-stemmed dogwood. Follow the broad path along the river bank. This is a short but very pleasant section, and allows an escape from the heavy traffic on Waterside Road. When the path ends at the houses, turn right and cross Waterside Road to gain access to the Luggie Park. On crossing at this point, the entrance to the park is partially obscured by shrubbery, but can be located next to the street light.

The Luggie Park is an attractive, landscaped area, stretching from this point round to Kirkintilloch town centre, with the river Luggie as its main focus. As you walk along the paths you will see many planted trees such as grey alder and white poplar. Follow the path along the riverbank until it leads out on to the pavement of Redbrae Road, and after 50 yards re-enters the park. Alternatively, continue on over the grass, past the trees, until the footpath reappears.

Another 50 yards on, the path forks. Bear right; do not cross the footbridge. Follow the path through the trees until it leads into the open, keeping to the edge of the woods. Further along, the path forks again; bear right, still keeping to the edge of the woods (the other path can be seen leading to Townhead). As you proceed, ignore the wooden steps on the right, and continue past the children's play area. The path ends here, but cross the grass to the path that can be seen straight ahead and which again follows the tree-line before coming to a footbridge over the Luggie. On crossing the bridge, the path immediately on the right leads under the Forth and Clyde Canal to the Eastside, and connects with the Strathkelvin Railway Walkway. The path ahead leads up and onto the canal embankment, where a left turn leads into Kirkintilloch town centre.

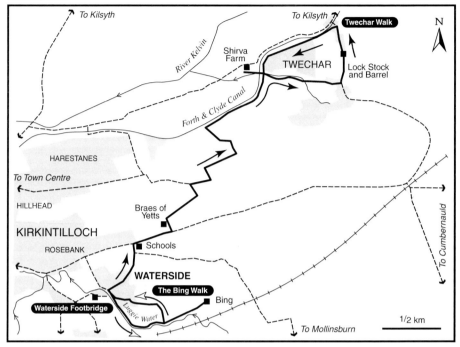

The Waterside Bing

Approximate walking time ten minutes, with extra time spent admiring the views

Because it has been there for so long, and can be seen throughout the District, we tend to take the Waterside Bing for granted, but a visit to this vantage point on a clear day can be very rewarding.

Starting from Bankhead Road, do not cross the footbridge but turn upstream along the riverbank until the path reaches the bridge mentioned in the Luggie Water walk. As you walk beside the river you will pass clumps of sweet cicely with its attractive aniseed smell. This plant has many culinary uses. Continue past the bridge, with the perimeter railings of a small industrial estate on your left. The path then makes its way through trees until it emerges into an open area. At the far end of this open area, watch for the fork in the path. Take the left fork, which is less prominent but can be seen to lead towards the bing. The top is easily reached within a few minutes. We do not think of bings as botanically rich areas. However, there are plants that specialise in these areas, such as helleborines, weld, great mullein, golden rod, roses and the flattened meadow grass. Once there, the views are superb in every direction.

To return, descend and retrace the route back to the bridge. Turn right, taking the path alongside the perimeter railings of the industrial estate and slightly uphill, passing three houses. On reaching the miners' road, turn left back to Waterside. After passing the bus depot, walk diagonally across the bus turning circle to the top of Bankhead Road, and from there downhill to the footbridge.

Waterside to Twechar

About an hour, round trip

Starting at the footbridge over the Luggie Water, cross Bankhead Road and turn left, then right into Back O'Dykes Road, noting the village hall. There is no road sign at the corner. Next there is an open grassy area with a footpath leading straight ahead to Moss Road, which becomes a footpath leading to an unnamed road. Turn left, passing St Agatha's School on the corner of the B8048 from Kirkintilloch to Twechar. Cross here and turn right, keeping on the pavement until you reach Langmuirhead Road on the left. Keep on this road, passing Braes O'Yetts Farm on the left, where the road bends to the right. At a T-junction, turn right on to St Flanan Road, which winds round in a north-westerly direction to reach the off-side canal bank. There are signs of former industrial activity on the right. Turn right and keep on the canal side towards Twechar. There is a good path through the trees to the right, but pass this and go onto Shirva Glen, to see the canal architecture, taking the Board Burn under the canal. There is a pathway to go under and back. Note the masons' marks on the stones, presumably made to ensure payment. Now take the path upstream to Twechar Park, leaving by a short opening between the buildings opposite the sports building (closed at time of writing) to reach main Street. Turn left uphill to the Lock Stock and Barrel Inn, the start of the Twechar walks.

Either return by the same route or turn right at the Inn through the village down to the canal. Turning left on the off-side path leads back to Shirva Glen on the outward route.

57

Community history – Don Martin

Twechar

There is a long history of mining activity in the Twechar locality, but it was not until the coming of William Baird & Co. to the area about 1860 that a close-knit mining community was created. Pits were sunk at Twechar and Gartshore and a row of workers' houses was built on the south bank of the canal, just east of Twechar Bridge. This soon proved inadequate and about 1880 the Barrhill Rows were constructed at right angles to Main Street, on its western side. At first there were four rows, supplemented by two more about 1900, by which date the total number of dwellings in the rows was 160. The row nearest the canal included a Gartsherrie Co-operative shop, and accordingly was know as the "Store Row". At first the houses had no sanitation and were lit by paraffin lamps. Communal wash houses were provided at intervals along each row. Most of the houses were of the two-apartment (room and kitchen) variety.

A great improvement was made in 1925, when Baird & Co. provided good-quality modern housing for their mine workers at Burnbrae, Annieston, Sunnyhill and adjacent streets. There were 200 dwellings in all, some two-apartment and some three-apartment, built in two-story blocks of four. They were provided with bathrooms and electric lighting. When these houses were built the old row on the south bank of the canal was demolished. The Barrhill Rows, however, lasted until 1957. The Baird houses of 1925 are still in use today. Later housing was provided by Dunbartonshire County Council at MacDonald Crescent (1939), Alexander Avenue (1948) and Kelvin View (about 1955).

The coal mining industry begun by the Bairds in the 1860s lasted for just over a century. Twechar No.1 Pit, on the north bank of the canal to the east of Twechar Bridge, closed in 1964, while Gartshore 9/11, the very last colliery in the area, was shut down in 1968. Thereafter some Twechar men travelled each day to collieries such as Bedlay and Cardowan in Lanarkshire, until they too were closed, during the early 1980s.

Baird & Co. provided rail connections to their local pits at an early date, but for many years much of their coal was transported to market by canal boat. During the 1860s the canal company permitted Baird & Co. to place a railway swing bridge over the canal, a short distance to the west of Twechar road bridge, for the purpose of forming a connection between collieries on either side of the canal. As part of the deal the coal company agreed to transport a proprtion of its coal by canal, although this requirement lapsed early in the twentieth century. However, the swing bridge continued in use until the mid-1960s, its hand-winding apparatus having been made redundant on 1 January 1963, when the canal closed.

The reopening of the Forth and Clyde Canal, in May 2001, brings with it great opportunities for the development of Twechar, which lies close to the canal's half-way point.

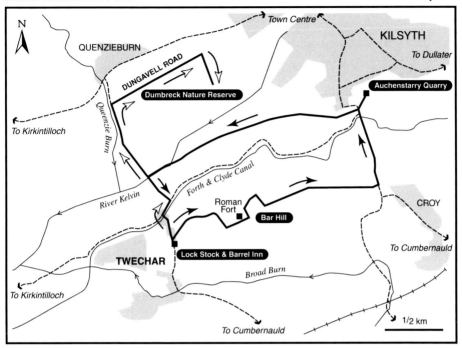

Twechar, Lock Stock and Barrel Inn

How to get there. Walk from Waterside, as described, or from Kirkintilloch along the canal towpath. Bus from Kirkintilloch.

Bar Hill and Auchenstarry Quarry

About two and a half hours

Turn right and right again up the track signposted to Bar Hill. It is fairly steep but short, and quite soon affords good views over to the Campsies and back along the Kelvin valley. The lane can be a good area to see crows – jackdaws, magpies, rooks and carrion crows. In the autumn when the oak trees are in fruit you can hear and see the jays quarrelling over the acorn harvest. Under the birch trees the fly agaric mushroom is found in the autumn. This is the red toadstool with white spots that is depicted in fairy-tale books. It is poisonous but is reputed to have been consumed by the Vikings prior to pillaging and misbehaving on their raiding parties. Near the end of the track, where on the right there is a concrete-roofed water-storage tank, turn left through a kissing gate on to another track leading to Bar Hill, a Roman fort on the Antonine Wall. This is well labelled as to the parts of the layout. The almost all-round view (mature woodland to the south) is over Glasgow to the west and, on a clear day, Arran to the south-west.

Walk on eastwards after the fort down a short dip and up to the top of the rise to the trig point. This is the nearest and lowest in Strathkelvin but was not available when Strathkelvin Ramblers were applying to the Ordnance Survey to adopt a trig point, so Holehead was adopted instead, and is being well maintained.

Return to the dip, turn left and walk down the broad, beautifully cut ride, which perhaps led to the Roman commandant's quarters; there is a level area and ruins of buildings. In the distance may be seen the trace of the Wall going over Croy Hill, the only part of the Wall not requiring a ditch, the north face of the hill being so precipitous. The cut grass gives way to a well made track, though it is muddy in places, ending at the Airdrie-to-Kilsyth road (B802). Cross the road with care and turn left downhill to where the new road skirts round the buildings and goes over both the Forth and Clyde Canal and the River Kelvin. On the right is a canal basin housing canal maintenance vessels and pleasure craft. Now leave this on the right to visit Auchenstarry Quarry, parkland with picnic tables, a pool with fish rising and surrounded by cliffs, sometimes used for climbing training. The Local Authority have planted shrubs around the parking area. There are whitebeams, which are a good source of autumn berries for the thrush family. As the winter closes in, the bright white fruit of the snowberry brighten up a dull afternoon, as well as providing food for birds.

Now cross over the road and find the track on the right bank of the Kelvin and follow it along, passing a community woodland on the right, planted by the Central Scotland Woodland Trust. Crossing the Garrel Burn where it joins the Kelvin, the track narrows and goes over the river by a footbridge, and soon joins Gavell Road coming from the main Kilsyth-to-Kirkintilloch road (A803). Turn left and then right at the road from Croy to Twechar, back to the bridge, over the canal and up to the starting point.

Dumbreck Local Nature Reserve

About an hour – more if time is taken to explore the Reserve, including two lochans, un-named on the map

Leave the Lock, Stock and Barrel Inn and turn right down to the canal. Cross it and the road, turn right and almost immediately turn left towards Kilsyth, between two industrial establishments. Go on down this road, passing on the right the signpost marked Footpath to Kilsyth. There is a new bridge over the River Kelvin, replacing the old one that was washed away in recent floods, causing the tragic death of two young men. After a short distance cross the old bridge over a dismantled railway line and then take the turning to the right, Dungavell Road, signed "no through road for vehicles". After a few houses are passed on the left there is a gate across the road, with pedestrian access on the left. Immediately after that, the road widens and has recently been resurfaced, presumably in anticipation of more new factories being built. There is one already established, on the right. After this, on the right is a well established woodland, one of several in the Nature Reserve. At the end of the wood is an entrance to the Dumbreck Local Nature Reserve. Go through the wicket gate, with the wood to the right, and you soon reach a metalled track leading uphill to a second area of woodland, the highest point of the Reserve.

The Reserve has a rich variety of habitats in which you can find water plants, emergent vegetation and, on the reclaimed bing areas, plants that are more suited to drier areas. The plants include bog stitchwort, fat hen, knotgrass, mouse-ear hawkweed, meadow buttercup, common valerian, great willow herb, yellow rattle, changing forget-me-not, cat's ear, common spotted orchid, thyme-leaved speedwell, angelica, cuckooflower, selfheal, colt's foot and fairy flax. In summer the following grasses are to be found: false oat, crested dog's tail, marsh fox-tail, sweet vernal, creeping fescue and cocksfoot. Sedges are represented by the carnation and glaucous sedges. There are several tree species including the grey alder, which is often found in areas of rehabilitation. There is a good population of waterfowl including mallard, widgeon, mute swan, coot, teal, lesser black-backed gulls and heron. Foxes, rabbits, brown hares and roe deer can also be seen.

At the time of writing there is a major pipeline project in progress, so the return route is by the same way. When the pipeline is complete, cross the Reserve to join the footpath from Kilsyth back to the road, so returning to the hotel in Twechar.

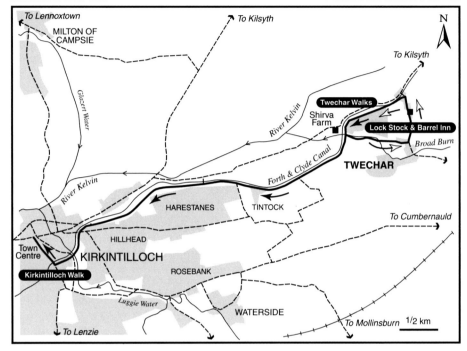

Twechar Parks and Board Burn

About an hour

Cross the road and turn right at the Chacuterie, going down to the canal, passing the Miners' Welfare Club on the left. Just before reaching the canal, turn left on to a path that leads to the first park and joins the bus route through Twechar. The park areas comprise extensive areas of grassland which are worth looking at for waxcap mushrooms – unless the Local Authority grass cutters have got there before you. In the winter time especially, these areas are good for thrushes. Look out for redwings and fieldfare. As this road bends to the left, keep straight on, on a wide track behind the houses. When the line of houses bends to the left, the path forks. Take the left fork, down steps to a bridge over the Board Burn. The tunnel for the burn to go under the canal is worth exploring; it is a good example of the thoroughness of canal construction. Cross the footbridge and turn left up a track on the left bank of the burn flowing through Shirva Glen. There are one or two tracks on the right leading back to the towpath, then one on the right leading on to a housing scheme over the second park. Keep to the main path, coming to a church on the left, the Twechar Community Centre on the right, the Twechar Primary School further over on the right and the Twechar Parish Church on the left. Go between the church and the manse to the road from Twechar to Cumbernauld and Kirkintilloch. At this point turn left up the hill to the Quarry Inn, passing on the left a third park.

Twechar to Kirkintilloch

About two hours round trip

Cross the road and turn right at the Chacuterie, going down to the canal, passing the Miners' Welfare Club on the left. Just before reaching the canal, turn left on to a path that leads to the first park and joins the bus route through Twechar. As this road bends to the left keep straight, on a wide track behind the houses. When the line of houses bends to the left, the path forks. Take the right fork leading up to the path along the south bank of the canal. There is extensive evidence of former industrial activity, now well covered by new growth. After a while you come to the village of Tintock, served by buses to Kirkintilloch. The path becomes a road, and soon bends to the right and goes under the canal. Now turn left up a steep path to join the main canal towpath. A short distance further a church can be seen in a prominent position on the left. On the right are some houses in what appears to be a hazardous situation from a line of very large, ancient beech trees. There also seems to be a risk of damage to the canal bank, but perhaps this is slight after over 200 years.

At the bridge, cross the road from Kirkintilloch to Harestanes and continue on the towpath under the bypass to the bridge at High Street. It is worth stopping under the bypass bridge which carries the New Lairdsland Road over the canal. There is plenty of birdlife here – if not in quality then certainly in quantity. On the bridge bearing ledges, large numbers of feral pigeons roost. If you are lucky you may see a peregrine making a sortie to collect his pigeon supper. Owing to local people feeding the ducks and swans here, you will see large numbers of mallard and mute swan. Some of the swans carry Darvick rings on their legs. These rings are large, to enable the identification numbers to be read at a distance. The rings are also colour coded to tell which ringing group has carried out the work.

Turn right and, if starting on any of the Kirkintilloch walks, go along to the Auld Kirk Museum. If not, return by the same route.

Community history – Don Martin

Kirkintilloch

Kirkintilloch was a place of importance in Roman times, when a fort was established there on the east–west barrier across Scotland nowadays known as "The Antonine Wall". This was built about AD 142 as a boundary line between Roman civilization and wilder territory not under permanent Roman control. For a short period it replaced the more southerly Hadrian's Wall. The departure of the Romans was followed by a Dark Age when little is known of Kirkintilloch's history, although the name "Kirkintilloch", in its original form of *Caerpentaloch* "The Fort at the Head of the Ridge", dates from this period. Light began to dawn again during the twelfth century, when the prominent Comyn family established a castle in central Kirkintilloch, with a parish church to the south (at the locality now occupied by the Old Aisle Cemetery). The Burgh of Kirkintilloch was created in the year 1211, and a local market was held weekly from then on.

In mediaeval times Kirkintilloch was situated on an important highway between Glasgow and the east, and indeed the town's axis was on a clear west–east alignment at that time: West High Street, High Street and Eastside. A bridge over the Luggie was established at an early date, and was of vital importance in keeping the highway open in bad weather. The parish church was moved from the Old Aisle to central Kirkintilloch in 1644. Improved transport links in the form of the Forth & Clyde Canal (1773) and the pioneer Monkland & Kirkintilloch Railway (1826) led to the establishment of important new industries, notably cotton weaving, iron founding and boatbuilding. During the twentieth century these all faded away, but there was an attempt to replace them with new ones during the period of Glasgow Overspill, around 1960. This met with very limited success, but the Overspill project resulted in the construction of many homes, in both the rented and the private sectors, with a consequent increase in the population of the old burgh.

The reopening of the Forth and Clyde Canal in 2001 has served as a reminder of the longstanding importance of this waterway to Kirkintilloch. Few canal buildings of historic interest remain, but the former Post Office building on the north side of the canal at Townhead Bridge was at one time a canal-side inn. A canal milestone is built into one corner. The "wide part" of the canal at Hillhead is a legacy of the canal's first western terminal, established in 1773. The aqueduct carrying the canal over the River Luggie (and for a time the Campsie Branch Railway as well) is an A-listed building and an important local landmark.

Other important landmarks at Kirkintilloch include St Mary's Parish Church on the canalside at Townhead Bridge, which replaced the Auld Kirk (at Kirkintilloch Cross) as the parish church in 1914; the Auld Kirk itself, now the local museum; and the adjacent Barony Chambers, which was built to replace an ancient Tolbooth in 1815. Kirkintilloch's market cross stood nearby until the same year, when it was damaged beyond repair by vandalism.

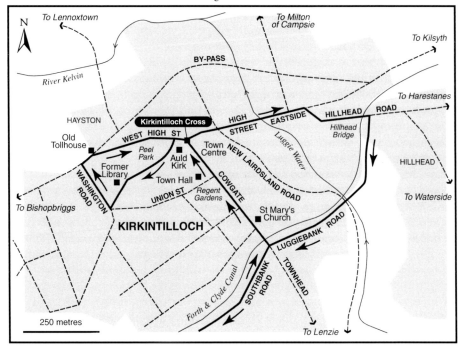

Kirkintilloch, The Cross

How to get there. Walk from Twechar, as described. Bus Glasgow–Campsie Glen. Local bus from Cardowan.

Walk through Kirkintilloch's past

About an hour and a half

The walk begins at Kirkintilloch Cross, the junction between Cowgate and the High Street. Ascend the Peel Brae from West High Street, passing through the War Memorial gates, which form the entrance to the park. There is no better place to begin the walk, for much of what remains of the more ancient aspects of Kirkintilloch's history is located here. You will see, enclosed by railings beside the western boundary of the park, a short stretch of the stone base of the Antonine Wall – a wall that was built of turf by the Romans in AD 142 or 143 to further contain the Caledonians and other northern tribes previously held back by Hadrian's Wall in the north of England. Looking northwards across the Kelvin valley to the Campsie Fells beyond, it is quite easy to imagine yourself standing on the furthest frontier of the Roman Empire in the mid-second century AD.

At the eastern side of the park is a pronounced mound of earth with a landscaped path running round it. This is all that remains of the medieval stronghold of the powerful Comyn family. It was William Comyn who was granted the burgh charter of Kirkintilloch by King William the Lion in 1211. The Comyn's control of local matters ended, however, when they fell from favour during the reign of Robert the Bruce. With the demise of the Comyns, the Peel area lost much of its importance, since the Flemings who succeeded them established their castle at Cumbernauld. It was not until 1897 that Kirkintilloch Town Council acquired the lands of the Peel and laid them out as a park in commemoration of Queen Victoria's Jubilee. The park amenities include the Perry Bandstand and the Hudson Fountain, both manufactured in 1905 by the local Lion Foundry, which then specialised in ornamental ironwork.

Before leaving the park, pause again to admire the outstanding view over the Kelvin Valley to the Campsies beyond. The Campsie Fells form an upland mass of hard basalt, while the marshy floodplain of the River Kelvin breaks the general pattern of the local landscape, one of lowland glacial deposits including drumlins. The park, and indeed the entire town centre of Kirkintilloch, stands on a drumlin.

Leave the park by the western entrance. Close to this on the right is the former William Patrick Memorial Library building presented to the town in 1929 by the town clerk, David Patrick, in memory of his brother William, a local Free Church minister. The library is now housed in a new building in East High Street, facing down Cowgate. Detailed information about the history of Kirkintilloch and district can be obtained from the well-stocked reference and local history department of the library. Important resources include the burgh archives and a large collection of local photographs.

Proceed westwards down Camphill Avenue; you follow the course of the Antonine Wall, which, though not visible, is just to your left. It is unfortunate that so little remains of the Roman settlement at Kirkintilloch. Although periodic excavations have thrown up pottery sherds and other artifacts, few substantial Roman remains have been found. Even the site of the fort itself is uncertain.

At the bottom of Camphill Avenue turn right into Washington Road. At the foot of this road on your left is the former Washington Inn, which was an old coaching inn but is now a private dwelling. By local vote Kirkintilloch had no public houses at all between 1921 and 1969 and none of the few remaining old inns have reverted to their former status. Facing you across the road is the old tollhouse, which is now also a dwelling house. You can still see, built into the wall, the slab showing the "scale of charges" for the use of the highway. There were at one time no fewer than six toll-bars located within the burgh of Kirkintilloch, but the last of them disappeared about a century ago.

Now turn eastwards up West High Street. On your left is the venerable Westermains Farm building, whose crow-stepped gables proclaim it to be at least 200 years old. It was for many years occupied by the Freelands, one of Kirkintilloch's old burgess families, whose name survives in Freeland Place. Immediately beyond the farm is a pathway leading off to the north. This is the remains of the old Coal Road, reputedly used by Lennoxtown-bound coal carts to avoid passing the toll-bar at the foot of the hill.

At the top of West High Street the steeple marks the former site of the ancient tollbooth where market-dues were paid and also the market cross (smashed by vandals in 1815!). Opposite on the left is the new library. Continue eastwards into High Street, which was a hub of activity in medieval times, cross the new ring road and descend to Luggie Bridge, a river crossing of some antiquity. Generally the Luggie Water is a docile water-course, but after heavy rain it flows fast and furious., hence a bridge was necessary here at a period when a ford sufficed for most river crossings. Medieval packmen used the east–west road through Kirkintilloch in great numbers and relied on the existence of the bridge to enable them to carry on their trade at all times of the year. Unfortunately, there were frequent complaints that the bridge had "fallin doun". The present bridge was much altered and widened just under a century ago, but rests on a very old foundation. An old milestone can be seen at one corner. Just over the bridge, on the right, is a memorial to Hazelton Robert Robson, a Glasgow youth who lost his life in 1876 while attempting to save a child from drowning. This memorial is a testimony to the treacherous nature of the Luggie in flood. The building beside the Robson monument is one of the oldest houses in Kirkintilloch. Around 200 years ago it was owned by Sir John Stirling, a local cotton mill owner.

Before leaving Eastside note the comparatively wide nature of the street. This street was once the focal point of an important local linen industry. A market for the sale of flax was held here. The ample width of the street, to accommodate the market, was even more evident before the erection of Liberal Buildings.

Now turn right into Hillhead Road and ascend to the Forth and Clyde Canal at Hillhead Bridge. This part of the road dates from the 1930s and was built to replace the steeply graded Hopkins Brae, which is on the left just before you reach the Canal. The swing bridge was opened in 1938 and replaced an old wooden bascule bridge. It has now been replaced by a new swing bridge, part of the Millennium Project. Cross the bridge and turn right along the south bank and you will immediately see the "wide part" of the Canal and the red brick buildings, which were formerly stables. These are the sole remains of the old port of Kirkintilloch, established at Hillhead in 1773 when the Canal arrived from the east. As the Grangemouth–Kirkintilloch (Hillhead) stretch of the Canal was the first to be opened to navigation, it could be claimed that Kirkintilloch was Scotland's first inland port. This port was established at Hillhead since the aqueduct between there and the centre of the town was still incomplete in 1773.

Passing on westwards from Hillhead, this aqueduct is the next point of interest. It is notable for having carried the canal over not only the Luggie, as originally intended, but also the Campsie Branch railway. When the railway was under construction during the 1840s, the engineers found to their delight that it would pass through the existing arch with a minimum of modification to the structure. The canal is again open to traffic and the railway has been replaced by a walkway, but the aqueduct survives intact.

Crossing the aqueduct you will see, on the other side of the canal, new blocks of flats on the site of the Lion Foundry. This, the last of Kirkintilloch's iron foundries, was best known for the manufacture of telephone kiosks and pillar-boxes for British Telecom and the Post Office. Another of Kirkintilloch's foundries, the Old Foundry, established in about 1830, was also there. These, and other foundries in the town, were deliberately built on the banks of the canal so that raw materials could be brought in by barge, and finished castings dispatched similarly.

Proceed along the south bank of the canal by way of Luggiebank Road, then cross Townhead and continue into Southbank Road. Down beside the canal you will see a pneumatic hammer from the now closed South Bank Iron Works, another foundry. The hammer was installed here in 1981 on the site of the former boat building yard of Messrs. J & J Hay, where a succession of the famous Clyde "puffers" was launched between 1867 and 1945. Further along Southbank Road was the South Bank Iron Works. Just beyond is the site of the terminus of the Mondland & Kirkintilloch Railway (opened in 1826), the first railway in Scotland to operate steam locomotives on a regular basis. It closed in 1966 and was lifted soon afterwards.

On the banks of the canal here is the site of J & J Hay's repair slip, opened in 1889 and closed as recently as 1961. At the west end of the slip the entrance to the former Canal Basin, filled in over 30 years ago, can just be detected. Coal from the Monklands was brought along the Monkland & Kirkintilloch Railway to the Basin and shipped eastwards along the canal to Edinburgh and other towns. In the Basin vicinity was another shipbuilding yard, that of Peter McGregor & Son, which was in business during the first two decades of the 20th century. Many different types of craft were built here, including tugs, barges, lighters, fishing boats and shallow-draught vessels.

Retrace your steps along Southbank Road, turn left across the canal and pass into Cowgate. There was formerly an old bascule bridge over the canal at this point. With the establishment of several bus routes during the 1920s and with buses becoming progressively heavier, there were genuine fears in the town that it would collapse into the canal, taking a bus and passengers with it. Eventually, in 1933, a modern swing bridge was provided in its stead. Following the closure of the canal in 1963, the swing bridge was itself superseded, in 1968, by the present embankment and pipe. Many local people were disappointed that boats could no longer pass under the road. An old canal milestone survives here. This part of the canal has again been opened to traffic by the construction of a new bridge, also part of the Millennium Project opening the Forth and Clyde Canal and the Union Canal.

The first notable building you will see in Cowgate is the impressive red sandstone St Mary's Parish Church, opened in 1914 to take the place of the "Auld Kirk" at the Cross. Further along on the same side is the Watson Fountain, presented to his native town in 1893 by Sir John Watson of Earnock, an important Victorian coalmaster. He was educated at the Cowgate Subscription School nearby. Opposite is the frontage of the new shopping complex. Across Regent Gardens to your left is the Town Hall, much needed when it opened in 1906 and still very heavily used by local organisations of all kinds. It is situated in Union Street, formerly one of the principal centres of handloom weaving in the town. A few more steps along Cowgate bring you back to the Cross, where you can conclude your walk with a visit to the Auld Kirk and Barony Chambers Museum.

The Auld Kirk was built in 1644 as the new parish church. It superseded a former building on the southern outskirts of the town at the Old Aisle. Whilst looking at the outside of the building, note the remains of the jougs (iron ring) which used to be attached to the wall beside the front door. Local offenders were tethered to the ring here whilst the congregation gathered inside. The surrounding graveyard also holds a record of local history and it is still possible to read many of the gravestones. On the same elevated piece of ground is the old Town House or Town Hall. Completed in 1815 it replaced the old Tollbooth which formerly stood on the same site. The building has three floors, with a steeple and clock tower. The ground-floor room served as both court room and council chambers. Upstairs was the school room, known locally as the "Steeple School". On a lower floor in the premises currently used as a shop was the local jail. Today this is the Barony Chambers Museum, with displays relating to the history of the town and its surroundings, especially its industries, transport and social history.

Credits

This walk through Kirkintilloch's past was prepared by Strathkelvin District Libraries in response to frequent demands for an easy-to-read "walkabout" guide to central Kirkintilloch. It is based on project work done by Mrs Angela Watson, a member of staff, when she was a pupil at Kirkintilloch High School. The school project was supervised by Mr George Reid of the Geography Department, who has contributed much to the final make-up of the guide. Each has kindly granted permission for their report to be quoted.

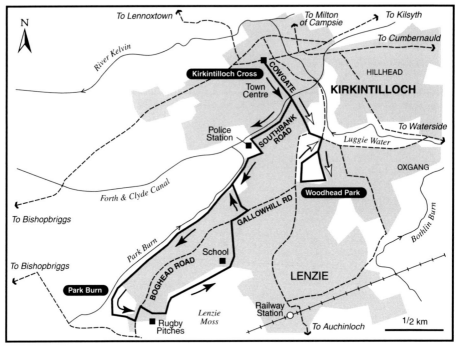

Woodhead Park

Leave Kirkintilloch Cross and, walking on the left side of the Cowgate, pass the fountain with the town motto: "Ca Canny But Ca Awa". On the right is a small park with a large shopping precinct behind. At the first set of traffic lights cross over, continuing along the Cowgate, crossing the Forth and Clyde Canal Bridge. Continue straight on past the gap in the buildings on the right that leads to the Co-op supermarket and pass the pedestrian crossing until a second set of traffic lights is reached. Cross over and continue along Industry Street. The narrow entrance leading to Woodhead Park is on the opposite side of the road. Enter here and stroll through a small stand of trees, gardens, greenhouse (open to the public) and putting greens. This is an ideal spot to rest on one of the wooden seats before walking forward to the left, towards the children's play area and community centre. Follow the tarmac path in front of the centre and turn left when it meets Parkview Road. Walk left to the end of the road, then right. Follow this until it becomes a path. After passing another play area on the right, the path eventually joins a wider path (disused railway) on your right. Join it by turning sharp right and return to Woodhead Park by this path. Walk over the grass to the tree area and return by the same route to Kirkintilloch Cross.

Park Burn

About an hour and a half

Leaving the Cross, walk on the right along Cowgate, cross the canal and turn right up Southbank Road, passing doctors' surgeries and the Registry Office on the left and the new education building on the right. Turn left, past the new Police Station and the first of the buildings of the Southbank Business Park. At the T-junction turn right and keep on until the road ends. Follow the path, with open grassland on the right and trees on the left. The path forks; the left branch goes down steps with houses on the left and, behind trees, the Park Burn. There are specimens of the guelder rose, which is a small tree planted by the local authority, now self seeding, owing to birds eating the red berries and spreading them about. In the spring the white flowers appear in umbel-like clusters, which have outer flowers that are larger and more attractive. These flowers are not fertile, and are purely as an attraction. An interesting comparison can be made between the low-growing ground elder and the elder trees growing nearby.

The next half mile or so is more open, with children's play areas on the left, and farmland on the right. Next, a Community Woodland is reached. Either take a left turn where the path goes up steps, or follow the path that bends to the left. Both meet at a wooden stile, at Boghead Road. Cross the road and take the first turn right, Heather Drive. Follow this to its end at an open grassed area. Turn left for a short distance to the entrance of a wooded part of Lenzie Moss. There are several paths through the trees; choose the driest and keep as close as possible to the houses on the left and gradually the going gets better and the ground opens up on the right.

Leave by an opening just past the primary school and go down Moss Road. Cross Gallowhill Road at the Elim church, turn right then first left and go steeply downhill on Park Burn Avenue to join the Park Burn path back to the Police Station and the Cross.

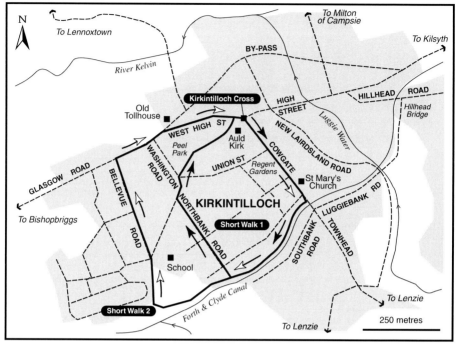

Short walks featuring the canal in Kirkintilloch

Walk 1

Less than an hour

Starting at the Cross, walk along Cowgate shopping area on the right pavement to the new Townhead Canal Bridge with its smart logo and lights. Cross the bridge and turn right, to see the old Forging Hammer from the former Southbank Iron Foundry. Return to the main towpath. There are seats on both sides of the canal at this point and a Canal information board. Across the main street there is also seating and a bronze plaque on a sandstone plinth, depicting eight former industries in Kirkintilloch. This was cast by the last remaining foundry in Kirkintilloch.

On the far bank is the Seagull Yarrow jetty and boathouse. Two boats there give handicapped people in the community trips along the canal. With the opening of the bridges at Townhead, Hillhead and Twechar eastwards and Cadder and Balmuildy westwards, these boats can now cruise further afield, giving a great deal of pleasure.

In this area, Puffers were built at Hays Yard and were launched broadside-on into the canal, with a huge splash to the cheers of children and locals on the bridge. There is also a slipway where boats were repaired. Immediately beyond this is the nearly hidden entrance to the old canal basins, where McGregor's Yard built small passenger and cargo steamers for home waters and abroad. The basins are now infilled, but one may be opened up again for a marina. Near here, the Southbank swans nest.

Nearly opposite here, there are narrow steps up on the right to the junction of Alexandra Street and Northbank Road. Walk along Northbank Road, turn right into Bellfield Road for a very short distance, and then cross at the junction of Washington Road and Union Street to walk up Camphill Avenue to Peel Park, a conservation area. There are only two houses in Camphill Avenue. On the left, there is the old William Patrick Library, formerly a private house, then gifted to the people of Kirkintilloch, and now once again a private house. On the right is Sunnyside House, with a beautiful garden. Walk through Peel Park past the bandstand or linger to admire one of the best views of the Campsie Fells. Walk through the War Memorial Gates down a short steep road to return to the starting point at the Cross.

Walk 2

Less than an hour

Go along Cowgate, turn right on to the towpath, continue along beyond steps with St Ninian's High School and playing fields up on your right until you come to a distinctive dead tree. The Park Burn comes from under the canal. With the concrete works across the canal on the left, turn right down a narrow path beside the burn, bearing right up a path along the side of St Ninian's School. Cross the junction of Roman Road and Bellfield Road and head down Bellevue Road to Glasgow Road. There is hardly any pavement, but it is safe, as this is now closed to traffic on to Glasgow Road with a barrier. Turn right at the main road past the fire station, cross the main road before the roundabout at the junction of West High Street and Kilsyth Road, and look at the old Toll Cottage, which is beautifully restored, showing the old toll charges. Cross back to west High Street and climb up to the Cross.

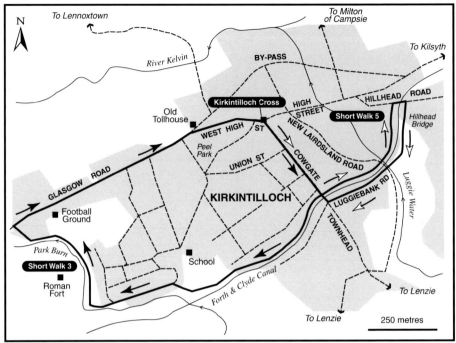

Walk 3

About an hour

Start at the Cross as in Walks 1 and 2 and continue along the towpath past the dead tree. Do not take the first path off to the right (this can be slippy) but continue along the towpath to the path down, just before the beginning of a line of trees. There is a jetty on the opposite bank with an ever increasing number of boats, called the Dutch Navy, as the Holland family own the land. You may be lucky to see the Wee Spark, a miniature puffer, built more recently at Bowling, or the Harmony Row, built locally by Sim Builders when they had a slack time; she spent part of her life as a scallop-fishing boat in Oban, and was called the Sea Witch, before returning home to Kirkintilloch. Between the canal and Campsie View, on the far side of the burn, is the site of a Roman camp. Now turn right, crossing the Park Burn by a wooden bridge, bearing left past an old quarry, then past the Rob Roy Football Club, to enter the cul-de-sac at Campsie View. The Park Burn flows into the River Kelvin. When you reach the Glasgow Road, turn right and follow the main road up to the Cross.

Walk 4

About two hours

Walk from the Cross, as before, keeping on the towpath to the Stables pub/restaurant, and go under the Glasgow Bridge. There are more boats operating from here. Between the Dutch Navy jetty and Stables there is pleasant countryside, mainly fields on the off-side – with perhaps the sight of a heron on the last stretch to the Stables – and trees along the towpath with views to the Campsies. Either walk on to Hungryside Bridge, or have some refreshment at the Stables and return to Kirkintilloch by the pavement past the Hayston Estate.

Walk 5

About half an hour

From the Cross, walk along Cowgate on the left pavement to Townhead Canal Bridge. Turn left down a steep ramp on the towpath, under the Nicholson Bridge, which carries the by-pass road over the canal. Next walk over the Luggie aqueduct, a single arch with iron railings, looking down to where the Campsie railway ran over the Luggie Burn. There is a good view up to the Campsie Fells. It is worthwhile going down the steps after the aqueduct to look up at this unusual structure. Climb up again to the towpath and walk on to the recently restored swing bridge on Hillhead Road, with its old lighting. Cross the bridge and return on the other side of the canal. First you come to the old Hillhead Basin, which may be improved for moorings for pleasure craft in the near future. From the aqueduct, look down on to the Luggie Park. Beside the Nicholson Bridge is an area where about fifty swans and mallards winter, fed by locals. After the Nicholson Bridge return to the Townhead Bridge along Luggiebank Road and turn right for the Cross.

Kirkintilloch to Twechar

About an hour each way

From the Cross, go along Cowgate to the new canal bridge and turn left to the towpath, going under the new ring road and over the aqueduct described earlier. Next is the recently rebuilt swing bridge for Hillhead Street, then it is straight forward to Twechar, with good views of the Campsies on a clear day. At the village turn right over the new basquile bridge over the canal and go up the road past the War Memorial to the Lock, Stock and Barrel, the starting point for the Twechar walks.

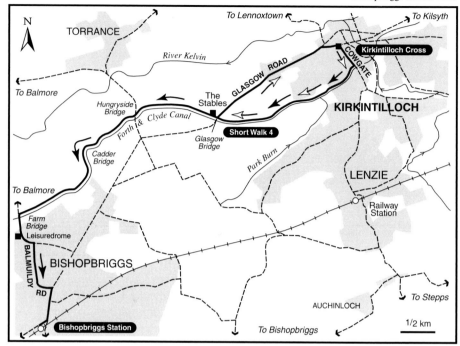

Kirkintilloch to Bishopbriggs

About an hour one way

From the Cross turn right along Cowgate and right again on to the canal towpath heading
west, and keep going past the Stables, Hungryside Bridge and Cadder Bridge to the
Leisuredrome, the start point of some of the Bishopbriggs walks. To get to the start point
of the others – Bishopbriggs Railway Station – from the Leisuredrome turn right along
Hilton and right again into Balmuildy Road and follow it to the main A803, Glasgow-to-
Kirkintilloch road. Turn right downhill to the Cross and the entrance to the station.

Community history – Don Martin

Bishopbriggs

Bishopbriggs shares certain elements of its history with Kirkintilloch and others with Lenzie. Like Kirkintilloch it was a roadside village on a major highway from Glasgow to the east, the line of which is preserved by Crowhill Road and north of Bishopbriggs Cross by the "Low Road" (less clearly seen since the building of "The Triangle"). Like Lenzie it enjoyed the benefits of a railway station from 1842, when the main Edinburgh & Glasgow Railway was opened. As at Lenzie, free "villa tickets" were granted to persons building large houses near the station during the 1850s (in Springfield Road). Unlike Lenzie, however, Bishopbriggs also had a fairly large working-class population during the nineteenth century, employed in the extensive quarries at Crowhill, Huntershill and Kenmure. Those provided the City of Glasgow with sandstone for its tenements and other buildings. The workers were housed in tenements at Colston and in the rows known as "The Diggings" close to Bishopbriggs Cross. Later, a significant working population was employed at Cadder Colliery and housed in miners' rows at Mavis Valley and Jellyhill.

During the twentieth century Bishopbriggs reasserted itself as a desirable place of residence for Glasgow commuters. Large villas were built in Kirkintilloch Road during the early years of the century, and there was further construction of private housing during the Inter-War period (although a planned "Garden City" at Cadder did not develop as intended). Only during the 1950s and 1960s did population growth take place on a large scale, with the development of extensive residential estates. The resultant demand for autonomy of local government led to the creation of the Burgh of Bishopbriggs, which lasted from 1964 until the Local Government Reorganisation of 1975. Local residents then successfully campaigned to be excluded from the new City of Glasgow District, and Bishopbriggs was instead located with Kirkintilloch, Lenzie and other towns and villages in Strathkelvin District, for the next 21 years.

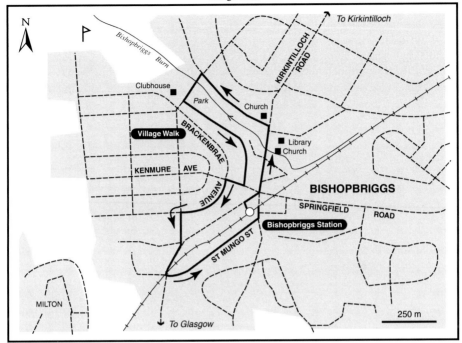

Bishopbriggs Railway Station

How to get there. Walk from Kirkintilloch, as described. Train Glasgow Queen Street–Lenzie–Croy. Bus Glasgow–Kirkintilloch. Local bus from Muirhead.

Bishopbriggs Station to Stobhill

About an hour

Leave the station at the booking office side, and go down the slope to Springfield Road. Turn right and right again into Arnold Avenue, then right into Emerson Road and left into Crowhill Road. This leads up and over the hill, passing on the left Huntershill House, the home of Thomas Muir. At the foot of the hill, cross Auchinairn Road, turn right and then as the road bends left before the roundabout keep on the pavement up to the lights and turn left into the road leading to Stobhill Hospital. At the end of the row of houses, formerly staff quarters, the entrance drive bends to the right and uphill. Take the driveway to the right. There are high ward buildings on both sides, then single-storey wards on the left, up to the top of the hill. This is the highest point in Glasgow, though not quite the best viewpoint, because of the very high blocks of flats, but it is nevertheless a good view on a clear day and worth climbing up to get there. Return by the same route.

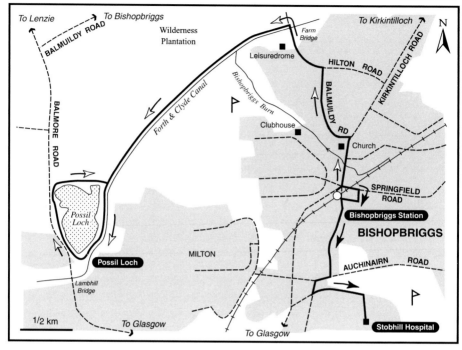

Bishopbriggs Village Walk

Less than an hour

Start from Bishopbriggs Station, platform 1 (Edinburgh bound). If you came by train from the east and alighted at platform 2, cross the footbridge and pause to enjoy the view from either end of the bridge. Walk down towards Bishopbriggs and cross Springfield Road at the traffic lights. Do not cross Kirkintilloch Road at this point but walk along the pavement on the right. You are now in what Bishopbriggs residents call "The Village" (see footnote). Pause outside East Dunbartonshire Council offices, called The Triangle, and look across the main road. This was once the tram terminus. Continue towards the next set of traffic lights and cross the road that leads to Safeway, but don't cross the main road. Continue along the footpath, which is lower than the main road. This was once the main road and was actually part of the Glasgow Inchbelly Road. Bonny Prince Charlie's army retreated along this road during the 1745 rebellion. Observe St Matthew's Church on the right. A burn runs under the road at this point and is crossed by the Bishops' Bridge. Unfortunately, the bridge can no longer be seen.

Pause to observe Bishopbriggs Library on the right. If time permits, a visit to the library is worth while, as it contains much information about Bishopbriggs. The building was opened as Bishopbriggs School in 1896, but was no longer required for that purpose following the opening of Bishopbriggs High School. In 1969 it reopened as the library. Continue to the next set of traffic lights, turn left and cross Kirkintilloch Road at this point. Turn right and take the second opening on the left. An interesting deviation at this point would be to continue to the third opening and sample refreshments on offer most days at Cadder Church Coffee Pot.

Back on route, continue along the path, passing tennis courts on the right. Stay on the upper path with a wooded area on the left. This is Bishopbriggs Park. A bomb fell near this spot during the Second World War. Continue to the end of this path, then turn left. Go down into Bishopbriggs Park, crossing the burn. In the park you will find lime, chestnut, sycamore, elm and beech trees. Alien invaders are represented by Japanese knotweed and laurel. Under the trees there are rosebay willow herb, broadleaved plantain, chickweed groundsel, pineapple weed, sow thistle and foxglove. Along the stream-side there is aquatic and emergent vegetation. Bishopbriggs Golf Course is on the right. Take the path on the left after crossing the burn, and stroll through the park. On arriving at the swings, bear right into Kenmure Avenue. Look for the telephone exchange on the left. This was opened in 1954, and superseded the old manual exchange that was housed in a tenement on Kirkintilloch Road.

Cross Kenmure Avenue, turn left and pause for a look at the War Memorial. You are now at Bishopbriggs Cross. Retrace your route back up Kenmure Avenue past Bishopbriggs Bowling Club, which opened in 1906. Turn left into Brackenbrae Avenue. Pass the Guide Hall on the right (Bishopbriggs has Boys' Brigade, Girls' Brigade, Guides and Scouts) and continue. Turn left at Brackenbrae Road, and cross Kirkintilloch Road at the next set of traffic lights. Turn right and cross the railway bridge. Take the path on the left, then fork left. The ground rises at this point, so be sure to pause and take in the view of Bishopbriggs and surrounding.

At the next junction take the left fork and go down a flight of steps into St Mungo Street. At the end of this street, turn left into Crowhill Road. Continue to the traffic lights. You are now back at Bishopbriggs Cross, and the station is on your right.

Footnote. Until the 1960s, the villages of Auchinairn, Bishopbriggs and Cadder, together with the hamlet of Kenmure, had been part of the Ninth District of Lanarkshire. The post-war building boom resulted in rapid growth of the population, so it was agreed to seek burgh status. The name chosen for the new burgh was Bishopbriggs and, in the years that followed, Auchinairn, Cadder and Kenmure were all but forgotten. However, when East Dunbartonshire came into being just over thirty years later, the names of Auchinairn, Cadder and Kenmure appeared as wards within the new authority – it is Bishopbriggs that has disappeared, from the political map at least.

Bishopbriggs Leisuredrome

How to get there. Walk from Bishopbriggs Railway Station, as described. Bus Glasgow–Kirkintilloch.

Bishopbriggs Leisuredrome to Possil Loch

Leave the station on to Kirkintilloch Road and cross at the traffic lights. Proceed along Kirkintilloch Road (north) to Balmuildy Road (first left after Cadder Church Halls). Turn down Balmuildy Road and turn left at Hilton Road and continue to Bishopbriggs Leisuredrome (you are now approximately one mile from the station). There are toilets in the Leisuredrome. From the Leisuredrome go across Farm Bridge/Balmuildy Bridge, and turn left on to the Forth and Clyde Canal towpath, heading west. Up on the right is the Wilderness Plantation. Unseen from the canal is the local refuse tip (now closed and grassed), and then the line of the Antonine Wall swinging north to keep to higher ground. On the off-side will be seen the rotten stumps of the Mavis Valley Railway Bridge. This stretch of canal path is the last rural walking before Glasgow. Several lines of pylons come into view. On the right, barely visible, are two entrances to Possil Loch, with extensive reed beds, a Scottish Wildlife Trust reserve and a Site of Special Scientific Interest (SSSI). It was designated as an SSSI because of the importance of its aquatic and emergent vegetation and waterfowl interest. The loch is surrounded by willow, scrubland, grassland, common reed mace, bogbean, great hairy willow herb, sneezewort, common spotted orchid and tufted vetch. Animals include roe deer and voles. On the water are coot, tufted duck, mute swans, teal and great crested grebe. In the reeds you may see jack snipe and reed bunting, with the occasional short-eared owl and sparrowhawk flying over. The small tortoiseshell butterfly may also be seen. It takes about half an hour to walk around the boundary, arriving back on the canal path. Returning by the same route, the walk will take about an hour and a half.

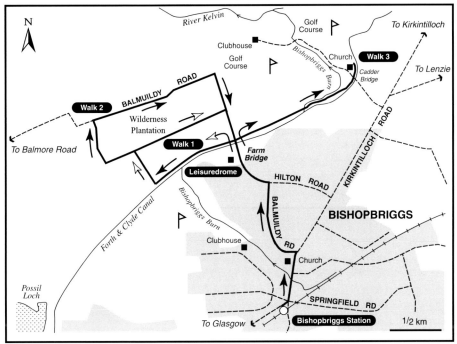

Farm Bridge Walks

Three short walks beginning and ending at Bishopbriggs Leisuredrome

Walk 1

The Leisuredrome itself is of more than passing interest. It was built in the days when Bishopbriggs was a burgh. A commemorative plaque indicates that the foundation stone was laid by Sir William Collins in 1971, and another tells that Princess Anne opened the Sports Centre, as it was then, on 12 July 1973.

Leaving the Leisuredrome, turn left and cross the canal by means of a newly constructed bridge. This bridge is a high-level bridge and was completed in 2000 as part of the Millennium Link. Traditionally, this is known as the Farm Bridge. The road and canal banks have been topsoiled during the bridge construction, with the introduction of such plants as viper's bugloss and wild mignonette. Other plants to be found are lesser trefoil, meadow foxtail grass and oxeye daisy. Pause on the bridge for a few moments and you may see swans, mallard ducks, coots and moorhen in the water. Continue across the bridge and turn left, along the canal bank. Just opposite Bishopbriggs Golf Course

83

there is a track going at right angles to the canal. It is easily missed, so perhaps it would be better to walk on the high-level path rather than on the towpath.

The path leads through what was once a thriving mining village called Mavis Valley. At the top is the Wilderness Plantation, once known as the Bluebell Woods. Turn right, and follow the path to the main road. Cross the road, turn right, and follow the road downhill to the Leisuredrome. This is a short walk, but it can be extended as follows.

Walk 2

Proceed as above until you reach the Wilderness Plantation. The Plantation has been a site often visited by the Glasgow Natural History Society over the past 150 years. The wooded area was planted about 250 years ago and comprised mainly oak and beech. There are many mosses and fungi, such as Chicken of the Woods, which makes a tasty meal. As it is a fairly ancient woodland, there are many interesting beetles and insects such as hoverflies, which spend their early life as maggots in rot holes in trees. Larger mammals, which may be seen, are grey squirrel, fox and roe deer. You then turn left, rather than right. Continue until you reach a single-track road. Turn right, and follow this road to the main road. Turn right at this point, and follow the road back to the Leisuredrome.

While a lengthy part of this walk is along a road, you are compensated by a fine view of the Campsie Fells. At most times of the year, it is possible to walk along the verge, or even partly in the woods. Look out for roe deer.

Walk 3

On this occasion, cross the Farm Bridge and turn right. Follow the canal bank, taking time to appreciate the wealth and diversity of plant life along this stretch of the canal. In the reedy margins of the canal you will find reed sweetgrass, yellow flag and branched bur-reed. In the canal you will see water lilies. There are white water lilies on the canal but the yellow lily is the most common. They can be differentiated by their leaf shape. The white one has an almost circular leaf whereas the yellow one has the shape of a lavatory seat. You can continue on the canal bank, but there is a possible deviation.

On reaching a small plantation, there is a track leading to the left. This track ends at Cawder Golf Course. Before that, however, the reasonably agile walker can leave the path and proceed right, down to a burn that flows through the wood you now find yourself in. Follow the burn, preferably keeping to the right-hand bank, and enjoy the flora and fauna for a while. Look for the remains of a lade that once served a mill. Sooner or later, however, you have to climb back up to the canal bank.

Back on the bank, turn left. You will soon reach Cadder Bridge over the canal. Pass the bridge, pass the first road to the left, and take the second road. Walk towards Cadder Church. The churchyard is most interesting. It contains a mort safe and a watch tower, both reminders of body-snatching days. The woodland around Cadder Church has elm, ash, hawthorn, beech, sycamore and birch. The under storey comprises a rich variety of plants including sweet cicely, which can be used in salads in both leaf and seed form. This is a good place for looking at birds. There are song thrush, blackbird, wren, willow warbler, robin and chaffinch. You may be fortunate to see a kingfisher flying along the canal.

Return to Cadder Bridge. During the 1939–45 war, there were wooden barriers at this point. In the event of the banks being breached by bombing, the barriers, and similar barriers at other points, would have been closed, limiting flooding. Fortunately, they were not required. Cross over, turn right and return to the Leisuredrome via a path along the south side of the canal.

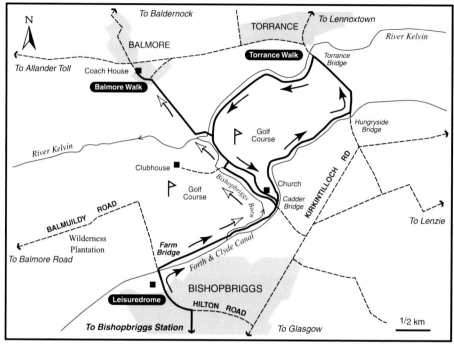

Bishopbriggs to Torrance, and return

About an hour and a half

Starting at the Leisuredrome, turn left on to Balmuildy Road, crossing over the canal by the Farm Bridge, and turn right on to the towpath heading east. At this point there are some old canal-side cottages, and a good view of the Campsies to the left. Soon there is a spillway under the towpath. The next bridge is Cadder Bridge just after Cadder Mill, hopefully to be restored as part of the Millennium plan. On the far bank there are more cottages. This is a conservation area. Just past the bridge there is a jetty with seating and an information board. On the left is the road to Cadder Church and graveyard. Return to the towpath, turning left with the Cadder Woods on the left. This is one of the prettiest stretches of the canal. Soon there is a narrow path up to the left, at the top of which is a good view over Cawder Golf Course to the hills. The other side of the canal is home to a variety of wildlife. Follow the narrow track on down to the towpath; turn left (east) to Hungryside Bridge. Do not go under, but go up to the main Kirkintilloch-to-Torrance road (A807) and turn left. Keep on the pavement until you reach the River Kelvin and turn left before crossing it. There is a retaining bank, though not a well defined path. Follow this down river, passing with great care behind the 16th tee of the golf course, keeping quiet and still if there are any players there. There is now a well defined path to the metal bridge over the river. Turn left (south) – this is a Right of Way – to Cadder Church. Turn right along the towpath to Cadder Bridge. Return to the Leisuredrome by either going along the towpath, or crossing over and turning right along a wooded path.

Bishopbriggs to Balmore, and return

About one and a half hours

From the Leisuredrome go across Farm Bridge on Balmuildy Road, then turn right along the Forth and Clyde Canal towpath heading east. At this point, there are some old canal-side cottages, and a view of Dumgoyne and the Campsie Fells. About 15 minutes after Farm Bridge, there is a canal spillway. About half an hour (one mile) after Farm Bridge, you arrive at the restored Cadder Bridge, just after Cadder Mill (hopefully soon to be restored). On the far bank there are old cottages. Turn left past Cadder Church. The road soon becomes a path – a public Right of Way – to Balmore across the metal bridge over the River Kelvin and on to Balmore. Depending on the season, Cawder Golf Club House can be seen on the left through the trees. Continue on and reach Balmore Coach House with craft work for sale. Before leaving the Coach House it is worthwhile looking along the hawthorn hedgerows of the old road. The roadside plants include feverfew, nipplewort, sticky willy, mugwort, daisy, broadleaved plantain, dandelion, hedge parsley, ivy-leaved toadflax and lesser trefoil. As you walk up Glenorchard Road on the right-hand side of the road on a wall is an attractive display of yellow corydalis, and further on the orange fox and cubs grows by the wayside.

Retrace your steps back to Cadder Bridge, where you have the choice of returning to Bishopbriggs along the open canal path or crossing Cadder Bridge and taking a wooded path on the right along the canal but on higher ground. There is a jetty near Farm Bridge, where you can feed swans. Return to the Leisuredrome.

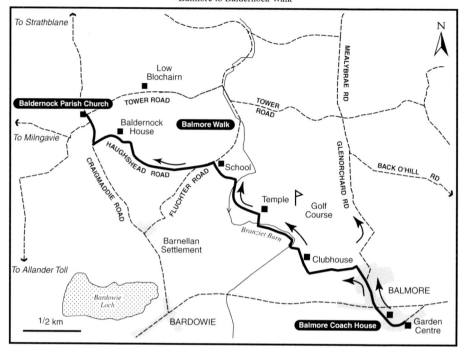

Balmore to Baldernock

About an hour

Start at the Coach House charity shop and tearoom. Before leaving the Coach House it is worthwhile looking along the hawthorn hedgerows of the old road. The roadside plants include feverfew, nipplewort, sticky willy, mugwort, daisy, broad-leaved plantain, dandelion, hedge parsley, ivy-leaved toadflax and lesser trefoil.

From the Coach House cross the main Torrance-to-Milngavie road and walk up Glenorchard Road through the village of Balmore. On the right-hand side of the road on a wall is an attractive display of yellow corydalis. Further on, the orange-coloured fox and cubs grows by the wayside. At the crossroads continue straight ahead on to Golf Course Road. The village of Balmore was at one time an area of many nurseries for tomatoes and flowers, but the cost of fuel meant a gradual closing down of these facilities. Soon the road becomes a way used by cars heading for the golf course and slowed by traffic-calming "sleeping policemen", making it less hazardous for walkers. Reaching the golf course entrance and the club house, it would be wise to use the lane at the back, but pause first to view the first tee and the eighteenth green and the many magnificent

88

trees. At the foot of this short path, cross the burn. Keep left beside the burn and watch out for golf balls from the eighteenth tee. There, follow a path across a bridge, often quite overgrown, but persevere, keeping to the left of the burn and arriving at another footbridge. Here is to be seen a house surrounded by a kind of stockade, up the hill on the right. Head for this. Pick up a path at the gates and start out on it. Take care to respect golfers holing out or teeing off in this area – an open area at the end of some trees. Golf balls may come over a hill here, as the position is out of view of the players. In fact, a loud bell is used on the left to alert players that the course has cleared. It is for the use of members only! Soon the path leaves the golf course and ahead you will see the school building over a large field on either side. At the school go through and turn left. At the first junction keep right. The view opens out. Follow Craigmaddie Road; turn right and so to Baldernock Church, the start of the Baldernock walks.

Community history – Don Martin

Baldernock

Baldernock Parish is remarkable as a quiet, rural, unspoiled area of land, located entirely within a 10-mile radius of Glasgow City Centre. The few lucky people who live there can genuinely claim to dwell in the countryside, and yet they are able to reach the city in the briefest of time, by the shortest of journeys. This was the ideal of the nineteenth century settlers of Lenzie and Bearsden, until those places became so saturated with housing that their rural aspect was forever lost. The same might have happened to Baldernock, for when Bardowie Station was opened in 1905 an extensive housing development was planned, of about 500 commuter dwellings. In the event, only half a dozen or so were built at that time, with a few more in later years, and the local railway was closed to passengers in 1951. The busy traffic in commuters' cars from Torrance, along the Balmore–Bardowie–Allander road, serves as a reminder of what might have been. All other roads in the parish retain their quiet, rural aspect.

In his *Rambles Round Glasgow*, published in 1854, Hugh Macdonald wrote enthusiastically about Bardowie Parish. Bardowie Loch he described as "Bardowie the Beautiful" and asked "if a glance of it would not more than repay thee for a summer day's journey". Bardowie Castle was "an edifice of moderate size, somewhat timeworn, yet withal wearing an appearance of quiet cosiness and comfort". Bardowie Mill was "an old and diminutive meal mill" inactive for want of water at the time of his visit. The former Kirkhouse Inn, beside Baldernock Church, was a "comfortable public-house where refreshment of excellent quality for man and beast may be obtained". Balmore was "an excellent specimen of an old-fashioned Scottish clachan". Nearby he encountered some antiquaries pondering the origin of a square block among the stepping-stones across the River Kelvin. Their idea that it might be Roman was derided by a passing milkmaid who identified it as "Redbog's auld cheese-press".

Macdonald's Baldernock can still be recognised and appreciated today. The meal mill at Bardowie has long since been converted to a sawmill, but still retains its waterwheel. The Kirkhouse Inn beside the parish church is now a private dwelling. The stepping stones across the Kelvin at Balmore have been superseded by a footbridge. However, the three giant boulders on Craigmaddie Muir, known as the Auld Wives' Lifts, can still be visited (with appropriate permissions), as can most of the other parish features mentioned by Macdonald. At Baldernock Church the little stone building at the gate should be noted. This was built for local people to maintain a night watch against the depredations of "resurrection men" (body snatchers) keen to sell practice material to the Glasgow medical schools. The kirk itself has enjoyed some considerable fame as the setting for Graham Moffat's famous play *Bunty Pulls the Strings*, first performed at the Haymarket Theatre, London, in 1911.

Walks in Baldernock: Preamble

The parish of Baldernock is a roughly square area of about 2½ x 2½ miles of rural land east of Milngavie. It is mainly agricultural, with some woodland and moorland. It includes the villages of Balmore and Bardowie, and a number of small settlements. With increasing mechanisation over the years the farms have become fewer and larger. The farmland is used particularly for grazing, hay and silage, but also for some arable crops, and various diversification activities, including stabling and fields for horses. There are also two groups of smallholdings. Two quarries for brick making and an old lead mine are all now disused. The best known features are Bardowie castle, loch and church.

Baldernock is a popular area for walking, cycling and horse riding. It has a network of narrow, quiet country roads and a number of footpaths, some having Right-of-Way status. Balmore Road (A807) runs east–west across the area from Allander Toll to Torrance. It has a footpath but is not popular with walkers because it is a busy arterial road. To the south of Balmore Road, the land is flat and low lying (Balmore Haughs) and much of it acts as a flood plain for the river Kelvin and its tributaries. Although the Haughs contain some footpaths, these tend to be muddy and overgrown, and are little used for recreation. An exception is the Right of Way running south from Balmore garden centre to a footbridge over the Kelvin, leading to Cadder. A disused railway track also runs through the Haughs and it is planned to make this into a walkway and cycle track.

To the north of Balmore Road, the countryside is mostly farmland. It rises to the north, where it becomes moorland. It is in this area that there is a wide choice of attractive walks on quiet roads and footpaths. A few years ago these country roads were signposted at junctions, but the signs are flimsy and low down, and are frequently damaged or knocked down by vehicles, and some have disappeared, as have signs marking the Right of Way. The road network is complex, and a glance at the map will show that there are many possible routes, ranging from about half a mile to six and a half miles.

Baldernock Parish Church is a convenient starting point for many of the walks, but for others it increases the distance, and the starting point may depend on how far you want to walk. The present church dates from 1795. The watch house at the entrance to the old graveyard has a fireplace and was used to guard against the theft of bodies in the days of Burke and Hare. From the church or nearby, Craigmaddie Road runs north–south, Baldernock Road runs west to Milngavie, Tower Road runs east to Torrance and Dowan Road runs south and west to Auchenhowie Road (A807).

The following walks are a few examples of the wide choice of routes available. Walks 1, 2, 6 and 7 start and end at the church; 3, 4 and 5 start and end elsewhere. All the walks are circular, although 5, 6 and 7 link to surrounding areas and parts of 7 are along the pavements of fairly busy roads.

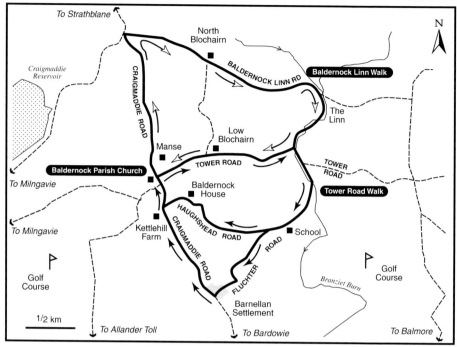

Baldernock Parish Church

How to get there. Walk from Bishopbriggs, as described. Walk from any one of the peripheral bus routes, e.g. Milngavie, Allander Toll, Bardowie, or Torrance.

Walk 1

Church–Tower Road–Fluchter Road, Haughshead Road–Craigmaddie Road–Church

About two and a half hours

Tower Road starts immediately north of the new graveyard. Head east along it, passing on the left a field (The Glebe) with a white house (formerly the manse) facing it. Along the roadside are roses which, in autumn, brighten up the hedgerows with their colourful hips, which were eagerly gathered in the last war to make rosehip syrup. At first the road runs uphill, passing North Lodge (right) and a beech wood. The first junction on the left leads to three farmhouses (Low, High and North Blochairn) and ends in Baldernock Linn

Road. The next road on the left is signposted to Baldernock Linn and at this junction Tower Road turns right (south) and crosses a bridge over Branziet Burn. Continue along Tower Road for 150 yards; it now turns sharp left. Continue straight on, alongside the burn, on Fluchter Road. After another 150 yards, this turns right (west) and crosses a second bridge over the burn, while a private road runs south to Wester Blairskaith settlement. Continue along Fluchter Road, passing Baldernock primary school (left). About 150 yards beyond this, bear right along a single-lane road known locally as Haughshead Road. This passes the farm track to North Bardowie Farm (right) and then a small area of infill at a gate on the left. This is called The Baker's Hole. At the gate is a sycamore tree that has made a remarkable recovery after gross injury caused by a fire at its base. The road then bears right, turns sharply left and climbs a short steep hill, after which it runs level with woodland on the right, and past an entrance to Baldernock House (formerly the residence of the late Andy Stewart, singer and comedian). The road runs straight for 100 yards and ends by joining Craigmaddie Road, opposite Kettlehill Farm. A right turn here brings you back to the church, after passing another lodge and entrance to Baldernock House. Over the wall grows a mature ivy, which is an excellent food supply for birds, as the berries do not ripen until winter, when there is a shortage of other food.

A slightly longer alternative to this walk is provided by continuing along Fluckter Road to its end at Barnellan settlement. Turn right (north) here into Craigmaddie Road, and thus back to the church. Past Boghall (left), the fields on the left are popular feeding grounds for pink-footed geese in late autumn and winter.

Walk 2
Church–Craigmaddie Road–Baldernock Linn Road–Tower Road–Church
About one and a half hours

From the church go north on Craigmaddie Road to its junction with Blanefield Road (A81). Turn sharp right (east) onto Baldernock Linn Road, passing a lodge on the left at the entrance to Craigmaddie estate and progress uphill, passing two houses on the right. The road then levels out and passes North Blochairn Farm and settlement (left). At this point a track (muddy in places) runs downhill to the right, passing High and Low Blochairn farm steadings to join Tower Road. This can be used as a shortcut back to the church, reducing the length of the walk to 1⅔ miles. However, it excludes the best part of the walk, which continues along Baldernock Linn Road, the highest road in the area, giving fine views to the south across the Clyde valley.

As you approach a wooded area ahead (the site of the Linn), notice a small concrete air-raid shelter beside the wall on the left side of the road. During the Second World War, lights were set up on the moors to deceive the night raiders into believing that they were the shipyards of Clydebank. The deception met with some success, for bombs and land mines were dropped on the moors, and in an air raid Lennox forest was set on fire. At the

Linn, the road turns sharply right. The area around the Linn is good for butterflies – small tortoiseshell, peacock, green-veined white and red admiral. The sparrowhawk hunts over the area and in the autumn the sycamore leaves show the common tar spot fungus. The Linn is a ravine formed by the Branziet Burn. It is approached by a broad track, which is lined by mature beech trees and continues straight on where the road turns sharply right. The ravine slopes steeply downhill on the right of the track. Within 40 yards, the burn has three waterfalls at outcrops of rock, and the third fall partly obscures the entrance to an old disused lead mine. To reach this, walk along the Linn track past the wooden gate and the group of three beech trees beyond the gate on the right side of the track. From here choose a reasonable slope down towards the burn until you see the third waterfall and mine shaft. This is easily entered without getting wet, and is about 5 feet high. The tunnel is complex, and about 25 yards from the entrance it is barred by a steel fence erected in 1972 after a group of Boy Scouts lost their way and had to be rescued by the police.

Apart from the mine, the Linn itself is a beauty spot, which in spite of frequent clean-ups is often marred by having waste tipped into it. At the time of writing, a complete set of bathroom furniture has recently been tipped into the ravine, from where it will be difficult to extract.

To continue the walk, follow Baldernock Linn Road, from where it turns sharp right at the Linn, downhill close to the path of the burn, to its junction with Tower Road. Turn right here and continue along Tower Road to the church (the reverse of the early part of Walk 1).

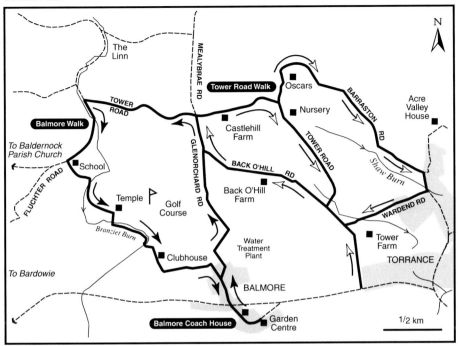

Walk 3

Balmore–Glenorchard Road–Tower Road–School–Right of Way–Balmore

About two hours

Glenorchard Road leaves the A807 at a crossroads, runs north through the village of Balmore and ends at Tower Road. Another road leaves the south side of the A807, completing the crossroads; this used to be part of the A807, but has been bypassed. It is known locally as the Old Balmore Road, and provides access to the Coach House, a well known charity shop with a small tearoom, Balmore garden centre, which also has a tearoom, and a housing estate at present under construction. The old road bears to the left (east) and rejoins the A807 after about 250 yards; its eastern section is a suitable place to start the walk. Before leaving the Coach House, it is worthwhile looking along the hawthorn hedgerows of the old road. The roadside plants include feverfew, nipplewort, sticky willy, mugwort, daisy, broadleaved plantain, dandelion, hedge parsley, ivy-leaved toadflax and lesser trefoil. As you walk up Glenorchard Road on the right-hand side of the road, you will see an attractive display of yellow corydalis on a wall and further on the orange 'fox and cubs' growing by the wayside.

Cross over the A807 near the crossroads and walk up Glenorchard Road, through the village to a second crossroads. Turn right and continue along Glenorchard Road, which then turns left (north) and passes the main entrance to the East of Scotland Water Treatment Plant. The road then turns right (east), runs straight for 200 yards with a belt of woodland on the left and the grounds of the water treatment plant up on the right. The road then turns left again, passing another entrance to the water treatment plant and runs north, with woodland rising sharply on the right and open meadows on the left.

A high wall on the left is almost all that remains of a walled garden in the old Glenorchard estate. The road then continues through fields to join Tower Road. Turn left here and continue along Tower Road and then Fluchter Road (see Walk 1) to Baldernock primary school. Turn left between the school buildings (notice the Victorian letter box in the wall) and continue between the school and car park (left) and Beanscroft (right) along a farm track (Right of Way), which also provides access to Temple Cottage. The track crosses over the Branziet Burn and turns sharply right, to run along the edge of the golf course (left) and the burn (right).

At this point look back to the left, and notice the 14th hole and, as you are still within range of the 14th tee, don't linger here. The track then passes woodland and the 16th golf tee (left). Again, look out for golfers and, when safe, continue past Temple Cottage, so called because there was a Knights Templar hospital in the vicinity. After passing the cottage, notice the 17th tee (right) and walk down the track to its left. If there are no golfers on or near the tee, continue along the track, across a railway-sleeper bridge over the burn, where the track ends and the Right of Way continues as a footpath with the fairway of the 17th hole and the burn on the left and a steep bank with trees on the right Again, don't linger here, as many golf balls land in or to the right of the burn.

Keep to the footpath on the right of the burn, ignoring two more bridges, beyond which the path is increasingly safe from errant balls. The footpath then continues straight on, crosses a fourth bridge and joins a broad track; turn right on this, passing a large shed, and cross a final bridge. Pass along the track, behind the golf clubhouse and through the car park, where the track runs into Golf Course Road, which, after left and right turns, meets Glenorchard Road at the crossroads in Balmore. Continue straight across and walk down through the village, crossing the A807 to reach the starting point in the Old Balmore Road.

Walk 4
Tower Road–Back O'Hill Road–Glenorchard Road–Tower Road
About 2 hours

Start at Tower Road, near its junction with the A807 and immediately adjacent to Balmore Park housing (at Torrance). Walk north along Tower Road, crossing a bridge over the disused railway track, and where the road divides take the left fork (Back O'Hill Road). At the next junction this joins Glenorchard Road. Turn right (north) into this and after about 150 yards turn right into Tower Road again. After about $1/3$ mile, Baraston Road joins Tower Road. To return to the start, continue to the right along Tower Road, but it is well worth walking 400 yards up to Oscar's Country Club by turning sharp left into Barraston Road. On the left, about halfway along, is the entrance to Barraston quarry, which formerly provided clay for making bricks, but has been disused for many years. The walls of the quarry have become naturalised with the growth of willows and other deciduous trees, and the floor of the quarry is now flooded by a small burn that flows through it. The overall view from the entrance is beautiful, particularly when it is not marred by tipped waste and burnt-out cars. Note also the fields on the right side of Barraston Road, and don't be surprised if you see llamas and wallabies; they are the property of Oscar's Country Club (formerly Barraston Farm), which provides accommodation for cats and dogs.

Either return the 400 yards to Tower Road or, if you wish a longer walk, continue along Barraston Road, past a group of smallholdings on the right, to reach Acre Valley Road at the north end of Torrance. The roadside verges are resplendent with nipplewort, meadow vetchling, yellow loosestrife, great hairy willowherb, yellow flag, germander speedwell, red clover, silver weed and mint. The alien invader *Rhododendron ponticum* also occurs. Turn right here and, after a few yards, turn right again into Wardend Road, which continues along a footpath (Right of Way) to rejoin Tower Road, a short distance north of the starting point. This alternative adds about 1 mile to the walk.

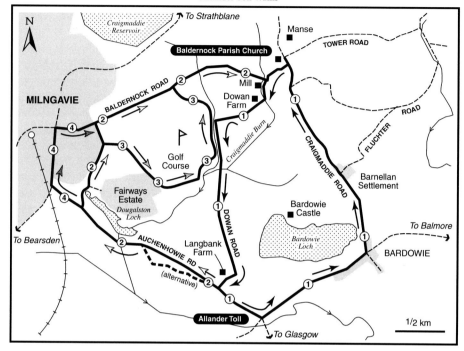

Walk 5
Baldernock Linn to Lennox forest
About three hours

This is a circular walk, of about 6½ miles, mostly on Rights of Way. It can be extended by a detour of 1 mile to a view point on Blairskaith Muir, and by a second detour of 2½ miles to Lennoxtown.

Starting at Baldernock Linn (see Walk 2), walk along the track above the Linn, which skirts the top edge of Blairskaith quarry, being separated from it in places by a strip of woodland. The quarry is of some interest. For many years it has been disused and is becoming naturalised by the growth of grass, various plants and trees. Parts of the base hold water permanently and are growing bullrushes, etc. In places digging reveals fossils – mostly of bivalves, but also brachiopods, crinoids and gastropods, and at least one fossil fish has been found. The wet floor of the quarry is also good for various amphibians.

98

The Linn track passes two other interesting features. One is a wigwam; at present this is occupied, but its future is uncertain. The second, a little further on, is a double line of mature but stunted beech trees, forming an avenue about half a mile long, running north at right angles to the track. The avenue was formerly the access road to a farm and ends at a raised, flat rocky area, on the right side of which traces of the stone wall of the farm buildings can be discerned. It is a fine view point. The avenue is not a Right of Way but its north end can be approached via a trig point nearby (see "Diversion", below).

About half a mile from the Linn, the track meets the rutted Mealybrae Road, a track that runs north from Tower Road. Here, turn left (north) and cross the fence by a stile. Continue along the track, which is often muddy, for 100 yards or so ahead. This used to be a public vehicular road to Lennoxtown and was lined on each side by a hawthorn hedge, scattered overgrown remnants of which persist. The track runs through grassland studded with reeds and hawthorn trees.

The tops of the coniferous trees in Lennox forest come into view ahead and the ground to the right of the track becomes increasingly uneven and hummocky, possibly owing to surface mining of limestone. It then enters the south-west part of the forest by a stile over a fence and runs north, climbing gently through a wide linear clearing in the forest. Ignore a lesser pathway to the right which runs east through the forest, eventually disappearing. Continue to a T-junction with a more major east–west forest track. A left turn onto this provides a worthwhile diversion (see later).

Meanwhile, turn right (east) along a hard-surfaced track that leads past Newlands, an open area of grassland in the forest containing two buildings and nearby communication masts. Here the track becomes a single-lane road, which leaves the forest and runs at first east and then north to enter Lennoxtown at Station Road.

About half a mile beyond Newlands, just before Muirhead Farm, a signpost indicates a footpath running south to Torrance. Follow this path through fields and continue past upper Carlston Farm (left) to reach Acre Valley Road. At North Balgrochan (just north of Torrance), turn right along Wardend Road, which continues as a Right-of-Way footpath to Tower Road, north of the old railway bridge. Turn right onto Tower road and return to Baldernock Linn by reaching the junction with Glenorchard Road and, turning right, taking the track up Mealybrae and then turning left on the track leading to the Linn.

DiversionAt the T-junction in Lennox forest, turn left instead of right, along a major forest track to the west. After about 400 yards, this track turns right towards Lennox Castle. Leave it here and walk straight on, along a lesser track, which is often muddy and divides eventually into two paths, both of which lead to a stile over the wall bounding the western edge of the forest. The right path passes a natural amphitheatre (right), where a concave downhill slope faces a hillock, on the top of which grows a small, perfectly conical holly bush. Beyond the stile walk along the rough footpath to a nearby trig point. This offers good views, and the top of the beech-tree avenue described earlier lies about 160 yards to the north-west across Blairskaith Muir.

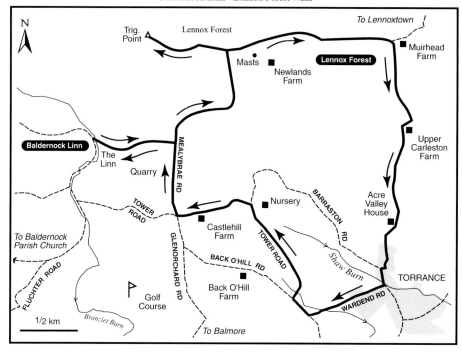

Walk 6

A circular walk from the Church to Milngavie and back (Woodland Walk)

About 1½ hours; 2½–3½ miles

Baldernock Road runs for 1 mile east–west between the church and Milngavie. It is a quiet, narrow road and much of it lies in the old Dougalston estate, which is extensively wooded but is partly open grassland, and now includes Dougalston golf course. Much of the estate is now owned by Esporta, a sports and leisure company, with recently constructed club buildings on the south-east side of Glasgow Road (A81). Two years ago, Esporta constructed a gravel walkway that starts at the club buildings, crosses Baldernock Road about halfway to Milngavie, runs around the southern edge of the golf course and rejoins Baldernock Road immediately before this reaches the houses of Milngavie. The Woodland Walk (here called "the Walkway") thus bypasses part of Baldernock Road and adds about half a mile to the walk. Its use is assumed for the return journey to the Church in this account.

The golf course is at present being modified, because part of it was on land leased to Esporta and the lease has lapsed. The land involved includes an additional loop of the Walkway that may not be permanently available. Accordingly, the description below includes only the permanent part of the Walkway; the additional loop, which is half a mile long, is described below (see Addendum).

On Craigmaddie Road, at the Church, a signpost to Milngavie marks the start of Baldernock Road. After passing the old graveyard and the house immediately beyond it (the Kirkhouse, formerly an inn), the road runs downhill to a junction, where it turns sharp right (signposted to Milngavie) and passes between the houses, the second of which incorporates Baldernock sawmill (see Walk 7). From here, Baldernock Road pursues a straight but undulating course to Milngavie. The roadside has a good mixture of trees and plants, including rosebay willowherb, brambles and creeping thistle, which is good for butterflies. Trees include oak, ash and hawthorn. The road crosses a bridge over Craigmaddie Burn, which supplied water to the mill, and then crosses Tinkers' Burn by a ford (with a foot walk). At high points the Esporta club buildings are prominent ahead and to the right, and a signboard indicates the point where the Walkway crosses the road. To the right, it leads to the Esporta buildings, where there is a map at the start of the Walkway.

Continue along Baldernock Road through pleasant woodland until you reach the first of the Milngavie houses on the left. Immediately before this, a few inconspicuous steps mark the end of the Walkway, and also the far end of this walk. Baldernock Road continues downhill between houses to end at traffic lights on Blanefield Road (A81). To return by the Walkway, climb the few steps mentioned above, entering a field with a prominent dovecote. The Walkway runs along the edge of the field, with houses nearby on the right, and divides just before reaching a wider track (used for golf-course tractors, etc.). This marks one end of the additional loop of the Walkway. Take the left branch, which continues along the wide track with a stone boundary wall of a ha-ha on the right. After 150 paces, a pond becomes visible ahead and the track divides; take the right branch and continue along the broad track. Ignore a branch track to the right, cross a railway-sleeper bridge over a ditch, ignore another branch to the left and continue until the Walkway branches off to the right, runs uphill and undulates, passing some fine oaks and beeches. Eventually it crosses a wide strip of grassland (formerly a fairway). As the Walkway re-enters woodland it turns sharp left at a T-junction, at which the additional loop (the right arm of the T) rejoins the permanent part of the Walkway, which descends through woodland and bears gradually left around the edge of a large area of grassland, then re-enters woodland and eventually rejoins Baldernock Road, where a right turn leads you back to the Church.

AddendumThe additional Walkway loop is entered by taking the right branch where the Walkway divides at the corner of the Dovecote field (see above) and continuing downhill through woodland with Milngavie houses nearby on the right. The loop crosses Finlay Rise (the access road to Fairways Housing Estate) and then runs between grassland on the right and Dougalston Loch, with Fairways Housing Estate beyond it. The loch is a nesting site for Mallards and other ducks, coots and water hens and usually a pair of swans. It is also fished by a heron and by fishermen. Various aquatic plants are to be found, including the white water lily, the yellow water lily and the rare hybrid water lily. The Walkway crosses a bridge over the outflow from the loch, continues alongside and eventually crosses Craigmaddie Burn and joins a rough access road to The Factor's house. Continue to the left along this road, ignoring a branch to the left, and passing the east-most Fairways houses to reach a point where a sign indicates that the Walkway leaves the track, running to the left and uphill through woodland, and rejoins the permanent part of the Walkway at the T-junction described above. Continue straight on here. For walkers taking the Walkway in the opposite direction (from east to west), the T-junction is not conspicuous, and if it is missed you will continue straight on into the additional loop. The junction is at the highest part of the Walkway in this part of the woodland, and the houses of Milngavie are visible ahead. Look carefully for the vertical part of the T, which is entered by a sharp right turn and runs across grassland on the right

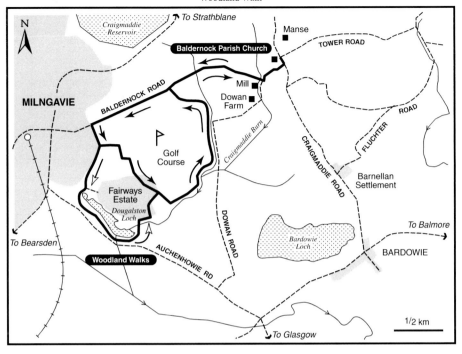

Walk 7

A walk along Dowan Road from the church, returning by Allander Toll and Bardowie or by Milngavie

About 3 hours; 3½ to 5½ miles

From the church, start along Baldernock Road, as in Walk 6, but on reaching Baldernock mill carry straight on along Dowan Road instead of turning right along Baldernock Road. The mill was restored, with a new mill wheel, about 30 years ago, and is best seen from Dowan Road. It is activated on rare occasions.

Dowan Road runs downhill and turns right (west), crossing a bridge over Craigmaddie Burn and, after passing Dowan Farm Steading, comes to the boundary wall of the old Dougalston Estate. Here it turns left to run south with the boundary wall and Tinkers' Burn on the right, and low-lying fields, which sometimes flood in winter, on the left. After crossing Craigmaddie Burn by a bridge, Dowan Road runs uphill and through Langbank (a group of smallholdings on both sides of the road and along a side road to the right). In places, Dowan Road provides excellent views of Bardowie Castle and Loch to

103

the left. The latter is used for dinghy sailing by the junior section of the Clyde Cruising Club. Apart from the usual wildfowl on the loch, there are occasional rarities such as long-tailed duck, smew and garganey. Rough-legged buzzard has also been seen in the area. Finally, the road turns right and enters Auchenhowie Road (A807) adjacent to Langbank Farm and about 300 yards from the Allander Toll. From here there are four return routes, all of which involve walking on pavements along fairly busy roads.

For the first route, turn left, and at Allander Toll (a crossroads with a roundabout) turn left along Balmore Road (A807) to reach Bardowie, where the castle and loch can be seen (left). At the crossroads, turn left to return by Craigmaddie Road to the church.

For the second route, turn right into Auchenhowie Road and walk about a mile along it to reach Finlay Rise (access road to Fairways Housing Estate). A part of the busy Auchenhowie Road can be bypassed by an old section of this road, which branches off to the left and rejoins the main road further on. Having reached Finlay Rise, walk along it for a short distance and, before reaching the Fairways houses, where roe deer cause problems by browsing on garden plants, look out for the point where it is crossed by the additional loop of the walkway. A group of trees in protective tubes will be seen (left), and a left turn up the additional loop leads to its junction with the permanent part of the walkway in the Dovecote field (see Walk 6) and thus to the Milngavie junction with Baldernock Road. A right turn takes you back to the church.

For the third walk, turn right onto the walkway where it crosses Finlay Rise and follow the additional loop to its T-junction with the permanent walkway (see Walk 6), leading back to the midway part of Baldernock Road.

For the fourth return route, walk left along Auchenhowie Road, past Finlay Rise, to reach the traffic lights at the junction with Glasgow Road (A81). Turn right and walk about 400 yards along to the next traffic lights, where a right turn leads uphill along Baldernock Road, with the church about a mile ahead.

.

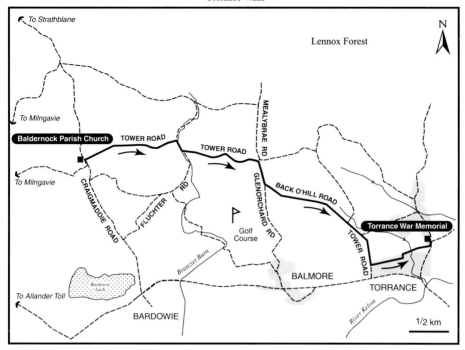

Walk 8

Baldernock to Torrance

About two hours round trip

From the church, cross Craigmaddie Road and follow Tower Road past Low Blochairn. After Blairskaith House on the left, turn right down Glenorchard Road then left on to Back O'Hill Road to rejoin Tower Road. Just before reaching the main A807 Balmore to Torrance Road, turn left into a new housing estate. At the far end of the houses there is a short path leading up to the Torrance War Memorial, the starting point of the Torrance walks.

Community history – Don Martin

Torrance

The village of Torrance is situated in a local area known for centuries as "The Eleven Ploughs of Balgrochan". The Eleven Ploughs were part of the estate of the Grahams of Mugdock (Milngavie). They received their name in 1630 when Montrose, the great military leader of the Covenanting period, sought to raise money for his campaigns by feuing off part of the Mugdock lands. The Eleven Ploughlands were feued off to local occupiers willing to pay a grassum (lump sum) on the understanding that their annual rate of duty would be held at a moderate level. Three of the Ploughlands were at Carlston, four at Easter Balgrochan and four at Wester Balgrochan.

"The eleven ploughs o' Balgrochan were acquired at that time
By eleven sturdy carles, as they ca'ed them lang syne"

The feuars originally held their land in run-rigs, running down in long strips southwards to the River Kelvin. In 1735, however, each feuar received an enclosed piece of land, in line with the widespread drive towards land enclosure at that period. Coal and lime continued to be worked in common, but ironstone rights were allocated to individual ploughland proprietors.

Some time after the enclosures of 1735, the village of Torrance began to develop. Some of the earliest inhabitants were "country weavers", weaving linens or woollens in association with local farming activity. Around this time, also, the extraction of limestone, coal and ironstone began to emerge as a local industry of some significance. During the late eighteenth century the improvement of local roads and the opening of the Forth and Clyde Canal, with a wharf at Hungryside, provided routes to market for local agricultural and mineral production.

When the Eleven Ploughs were feued off by Montrose in 1630, the large meal mill at Balgrochan was at the same time feued to a Robert Ferrie. Three hundred years later the mill was still grinding corn and celebrating three centuries of Ferrie family ownership. In 1933, however, it was closed and sold to a Glasgow firm for the manufacture of talcum powder. The mill wheel at Balgrochan was said to be the second largest in Scotland. It was cut up for scrap in 1949.

The canal wharf at Hungryside remained for many years as Torrance's principal link with the outside world. In 1879, however, a station was opened at Torrance by the Kelvin Railway Company and the village, somewhat belatedly, was linked to the national rail network. It might have been thought that Torrance would then have developed as a commuter dormitory for Glasgow, but the influx of new residents was slow in arriving. Indeed it was not until after the railway was closed to passengers in 1951 that commuting began in earnest. During the mid-1970s, for example, Henry Boot Homes built a considerable number of houses at Meadowbank and West Balgrochan.

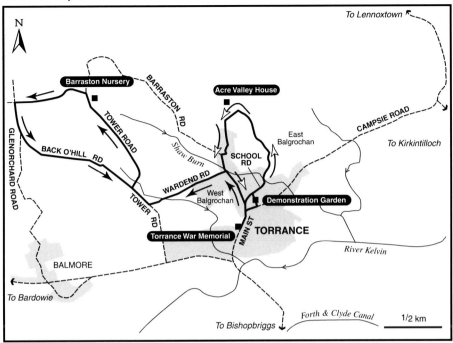

Torrance War Memorial

How to get there. Walk from Baldernock or Bishopbriggs, as described. Bus from Glasgow or local bus service from Kirkintilloch.

Torrance Demonstration Gardens, School Road and Acre Valley Road

About an hour, including the garden

Start at the War Memorial, cross the road, turn left and follow the main Torrance-to-Lennoxtown Road (B822) as it bends to the right. Soon, on the left, is the Council Demonstration Garden. The garden is very well maintained, especially in these days of Local Authority financial cutbacks. The centrepiece is the pond, complete with goldfish, water lilies and a waterfall. Adjacent to the waterfall are ferns such as common maidenhair spleenwort. Butterflies, dragonflies, damsel and hover flies occur in this area. There is a fine specimen of maple that is named red snake-bark maple. If the garden is open, spend some time there and go out of the back gate on to School Road. If the garden is closed, turn back down the main road, turn right and right again on to School Road. Follow this until you see a sign on the left to Acre Valley Road. Take this footpath and then turn left on to Acre Valley Road. Barraston Road comes in from the right, and then changes to West Balgrochan Road and then to Main Street, leading back to the War Memorial.

Barraston Nursery

About an hour

Start at the War Memorial in the main street (B822), go to the first junction and veer slightly left at West Balgrochan Road. At the third road go left at Wardend Road. This has some interesting dwellings, including the former home of George Pirie, the painter. The lane has both elder trees and ground elder. Although the species are very different, there is a similarity in the leaf form, which can be compared at this location. Comfrey and sticky willy, which is also known as cleavers, grow in the hedgerow together with sycamore, ash and hawthorn. Plenty of birds can be seen on the walk including crows, rooks, garden warblers, robins, tits, swallows and wren. Eventually this road becomes a fairly muddy path lined by trees, brambles and overhanging bushes, soon emerging at the bridge over the burn. Cross the bridge and turn right at the gate signposted West Balgrochan. This is Tower Road. Now watch out for the occasional car, tractor or horse! Continue on the road, passing Barraston Nursery on the right. At the next junction stay on Tower Road, bending slightly left and continue past Castlehill Farm on the left to a larger road junction. Take the left road, called Glenorchard Road. Note that the right turn, called the Mealybrae, would, after a climb, reach the forest track and Station Road to Lennoxtown. Straight ahead would go to Baldernock Church, about a mile away. Shortly after walking on Glenorchard Road, take the first left at Back O'Hill Road. This rejoins Tower Road and, signposted back to Torrance, the start of the walk.

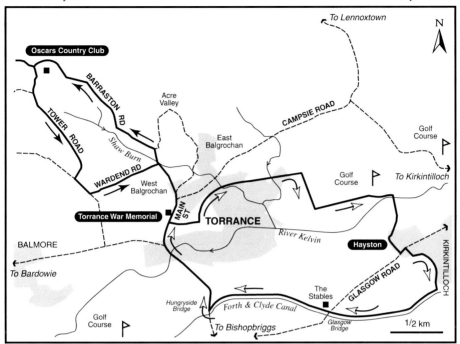

Torrance to Oscars Country Club

About an hour

As well as the familiar sheep and cattle, some unusual animals may be seen on this walk. Start at the War Memorial, head up Main Street, veering slightly left at Balgrochan Road. Go past Wardend Road, then turn left at Barraston Road. Stay on Barraston Road past Barraston House and smallholdings on the left. Before you leave the houses, note that some of the gardens have large beds of ice plant, which is a favourite of butterflies when they are in flower. The roadside verges are resplendent with nipplewort, meadow vetchling, yellow loosestrife, great hairy willowherb, yellow flag, germander speedwell, red clover, silver weed and mint. The alien invader *Rhododendron ponticum* also occurs. Soon after this is Oscars Country Club – no, not a roadside restaurant, but a sanctuary for animals, including llamas and wallabies. Previously this was a cattery and kennels, but that part of the business is no more. Having viewed the animals that roam free in a small field, continue, now passing a disused quarry on the right. Arriving at the next junction, bear left into Tower Road. Soon, at the path and indicator to West Balgrochan, follow the direction on the muddy path to Wardend Road. Finish the walk by turning right at West Balgrochan Road and back to the War Memorial. Apart from the final stretch on the path, this is a very pleasant walk on minor back roads, and should be clean and dry underfoot.

Torrance to Hayston

About an hour and a half

Starting at the War Memorial, turn right down Main Street and left up Rosehill Road. After it bends to the left and is about to bend again to become Cormack Avenue, turn right into a short path, then left on a larger track, then right and across playing fields to meet a dismantled railway line, where there is a notice stating that the path is for walkers, cyclists and horse riders. This point could have been reached directly from the War Memorial by crossing Main Street, through the park and down on to the path, but this next stretch is extremely muddy. Turn right, away from Torrance, and follow the path for some distance, to a demolished bridge. Leave the path and turn right, with Hayston Golf Course on the left. Turn left with the path, still with the golf course on the left, and go on. Cross the Kelvin by a footbridge and go on to the main Glasgow-to-Kirkintilloch road (A803). Cross with care, and go down a path through the Rob Roy Football Ground and turn right at the Forth and Clyde Canal towpath. Along the towpath you will find ivy-leaved toadflax on the walls, sow thistles, mugwort, ragwort, gowans, forget-me-not, germander speedwell and sweet cicely. If you have spare time, why not collect brambles for making jam?

Stay on the towpath going under the Glasgow Bridge and on to Hungryside Bridge, going under the A807 to Torrance. Turn right and get up to the road and go left, on the pavement and down past the farm on the left to the roundabout, and so back to the War Memorial.

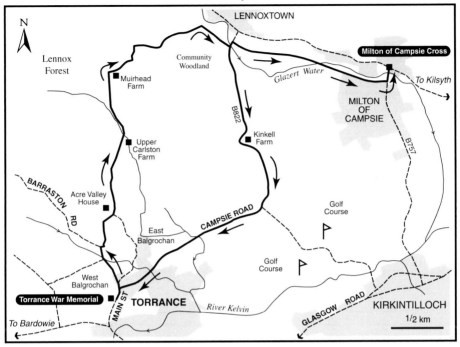

Torrance to Milton of Campsie

About an hour and three-quarters

(The alternative route takes about an hour and a quarter – three hours round trip)

Starting from the War Memorial turn left along Main Street. Where the road turns right to Lennoxtown, keep straight uphill past playing fields on the right to join Acre Valley Road. Near the houses, garden throw-outs result in yellow archangel and Japanese knotweed mingling with the wild flowers that include herb bennet, willow herb, creeping and meadow buttercup, and nipplewort. The trees in the hedgerow include beech, elder and ash. Many rabbits scamper about. Rabbits dislike elder, so if you are having problems with rabbits eating your shrubs, try planting elder.

The road now bends right and left and under power lines. At a left bend, at Acre Valley House, the road goes uphill. At time of writing, there is a large house being built on the left near the top of the hill. The road bends right to end at Upper Carlston Farm. Just at the bend, leave the road to the left and join a footpath signposted to Lennoxtown. This leads through several kissing gates and skirts the farm buildings, and goes alongside a burn, crossing it to enter a mature woodland. Where the trees end on the right, the path

111

turns to the right, away from the burn, which has come down the edge of the wood to this point. Soon there are fields on each side of the path, which goes on uphill to join Southbrae Road at Muirhead Farm. Turn right downhill. The road bends left then, where it bends right, take a partly metalled road to the right, downhill. Where it joins a better road, bear left. Soon on the right is a new Community Woodland, which can be explored. Before reaching the Railway Walkway, turn right on to a footpath and follow it to the B822 (Torrance to Lennoxtown). Cross over, turn left and then right, on to the Railway Walkway, turning right for Milton of Campsie. There are three large houses with extensive gardens on the left, and several paths and steps leading up to new houses on the right. The next points of interest are the circular archway of the road bridge and the remains of the former station. Here turn left and up to the B757 from Kirkintilloch. Turn right for the Cross, the starting point of the Milton of Campsie walks.

If returning to Torrance, go back along the Walkway to the B822 and turn left on the pavement, past the road signposted to golf courses and Kirkintilloch, later crossing the road to continue on pavement in to Torrance, turning right for the War Memorial.

Community history – Don Martin

Milton of Campsie

Milton of Campsie (or "Milltown", as occasionally spelled) is thought to be a comparatively modern name, although some of the local mills were hundreds of years old. There were at least three corn mills near the village, all attached to large estates, namely Glorat, Lochmill (for Antermony Estate) and Frenchmill (for Kincaid). There were in addition at least two other mills, both lint mills for the processing of flax for the linen industry. Perhaps it was Frenchmill, very close to the village, that gave rise to the "Milton" name, although this is unclear.

A great leap forward took place in 1786, with the opening of a calico printing works at Kincaid. This signified an important change in the local textile industry, from linen to cotton. Kincaidfield, as it was known, was soon providing employment for a large number of workers, and the village of Milton began to grow significantly in size. A second printfield was opened at Lillyburn during the 1790s. It was converted to a whisky distillery in 1826, but soon reverted to calico printing. Throughout the nineteenth century the local textile printing industry continued to flourish, but Kincaidfield closed in 1901 and Lillyburn in 1929. The works at Kincaid was demolished, but Lillyburn was converted to a pulp packaging manufactory, and continues to fulfil this function at the present time, although somewhat scaled down.

Milton of Campsie derived great benefit from the opening of a centrally placed railway station in 1848, on a branch line built during that year from a junction on the Edinburgh & Glasgow Railway, at Lenzie, to Lennoxtown. It served the village well for over a century, until closure in 1951, by which date road transport options had been greatly improved.

Visitors to Milton today should perhaps make a point of visiting Kincaid House, the ancient seat of the Kincaids of that ilk. So much of Milton's history is closely linked to that of Kincaid. It was the Kincaid estate mill at Frenchmill that seems to have given the village its name, and it was on the Kincaid estate during the 1780s that the calico printing industry, so important to Milton's economy during the nineteenth century, was first established. The owner of Kincaid estate during the 1830s, John Lennox Kincaid Lennox, inherited nearby Woodhead and combined the two estates. He built Lennox Castle to serve as an appropriate dwelling for the inheritor of extensive landed property.

When in the Lillyburn area visitors should remember the important McNab family who once owned the calico printing works there. Alexander McNab (1819–97) was responsible for the supply of gas and running water to the village of Milton and provided funding for the building of a public hall, in 1887. His framed portrait can be seen at the hall, in Craighead Road. Another significant local family, the Stirlings of Glorat, still own the Glorat Estate

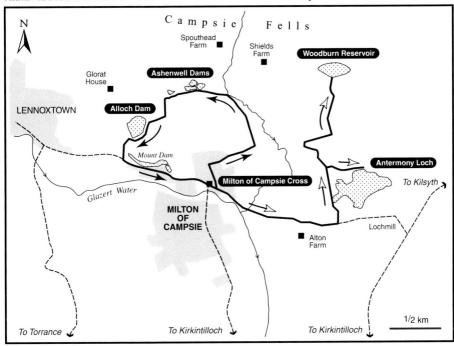

Milton of Campsie Post Office
How to get there. Walk from Torrance, as described. Bus Glasgow–Campsie Glen.

Milton Cross – Antermony Loch – Woodburn Reservoir
Milton Cross to Antermony Loch and Woodburn Reservoir and return, about two hours

Starting from Milton Cross, go east along Antermony Road, the road to Auchenreoch, keeping to the left side of the road. The pavement after leaving the village becomes very narrow (single file), and stops after a half mile from the start. Look ahead 25 yards to your right and you will see the footpath continue on the other side of the road behind the low wall that runs parallel with the road. After one mile cross the road to take the farm track on the left (directly opposite the entry to Alton Small Holdings). This farm track now heads due north. As you walk up the track you will see very natural hedgerow vegetation comprising hawthorn, ash and elder. Thrushes, including our winter visitors redwing and fieldfare, enjoy feeding on the hawthorn and elderberries. The hedgerow is also excellent for passerines. Look out for robins, wrens, chaffinches and tits. Swallows are a common sight in summer, swooping over the hedgerows. There is also a good population of common house sparrows, which are no longer found where they used to be common.

115

After a short distance Antermony Loch will appear on your right. The loch carries a good population of waterfowl. In the winter you can see cormorant, heron, mallard, pochard, tufted duck, ruddy duck, goldeneye, goosander and moorhen. In the summer you can see additional species such as little grebe, great crested grebe, mute swan, greylag geese, widgeon, coot, common sandpiper and gulls.

After crossing a cattle grid, a pathway goes off to your right, along the side of the loch to the jetty, used by anglers. You now retrace your steps back to the farm track. Turning left, you can return to Milton of Campsie, or you can turn right to continue up to Woodburn Reservoir.

Milton Cross to Ashenwell Dams and Alloch Dam

About one and a half hours

Starting from Milton Cross, walk along Antermony Road in an easterly direction past the Parish Church and War Memorial, and left into Craighead Road. Continue past the school and tennis court on to a private road, known locally as "The Back Road". After a short distance the road takes a sharp turn to the right and continues up a fairly steep incline for several hundred yards. At the top of the hill there are first-class views to the south. On a clear day, Tinto can be seen.

The road now takes a sharp turn to the left and heads towards the Campsie Fells. This road is also the access for two farms, which lie at the foot of the hills: Spouthead Farm and Shields Farm. Upon reaching the second cattle grid, turn left off the road onto the path which, after a short distance, passes the Ashenwell Dams. This is an area that is good for birding. There is a nearby sand martin colony and the martin can be seen feeding on the wing. Rooks can usually be heard in the background, and the higher pitched sounds of the buzzard hunting over the trees. As you approach the lochans look out for goldcrest and tits (great, blue and long-tailed). At the first of the dams there is a tremendous variety of plants both in the water and around the edges. You will see the reedmace or false bullrush. There was a painting entitled "Moses in the Bullrushes" that wrongly called the reedmace a bullrush. In order to satisfy the botanists the reedmace was called by some the false bullrush, as the true bullrush is a different plant altogether. On the water you may be fortunate to see coot, moorhen and little grebe.

The path continues over a stile and down the right side of a field bounded by a dry stane dyke. At the bottom, take another stile over the dry stane dyke, and then cross the footbridge into a small wood. The path continues through the wood and out at the side of Alloch Dam, which is an excellent area for fungi. The colourful caps of russulas and milkcaps abound in season. If you are not an expert mycologist, it is best to buy your mushrooms for dinner in the supermarket. Back on the path you may see the following waterfowl on the dam in winter: heron, mallard, tufted duck, goldeneye, goosander, moorhen and coot. In summer, in addition, you may see little grebe, mute swan and ruddy duck.

Follow the path round the dam, over the wooden bridge, and on to a track. Follow the track down, and then left; after a short distance you will reach the main road. Turn left and return to Milton Cross.

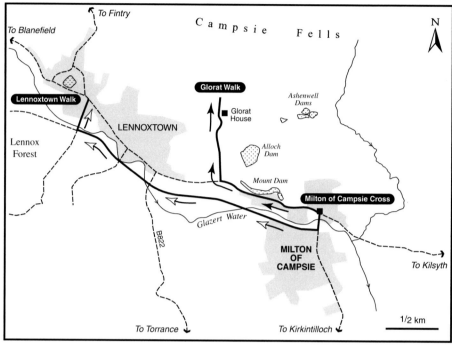

Milton Cross – Glorat – Lennoxtown

About 45 minutes

Starting from Milton Cross, turn left on to Campsie Road heading west to Lennoxtown. Keep to the pavement on your right. As you walk along the pavement it is worth examining the wall that runs alongside the path for plants such as wall lettuce and biting stonecrop. The driveway (on your right) to Glorat House is little over half a mile from Milton Cross and just round the bend from the traffic de-restriction sign. The track you follow is just past the driveway entrance and runs alongside it. This track will take you past a lodge house. On the left of the path there is a wet ditch where you can find the pink flowers of the attractive herb-robert among a mass of sweet cicely, which gives off a sweet aniseed perfume and can be used for culinary purposes. On the other side of the track can be seen rhododendron, which is a species alien to Scotland with few predators, with the result that large areas of forest land are covered with it to the detriment of the local plants and insects. Other species to be found here are horse chestnut, ash, lime and sycamore, with a good example of sessile oak.

At the brow of the hill, Alloch Dam is on your right. Continue on the track, passing through a small woodland. Shortly, you will be able to see part of Glorat House behind a large wall. You soon exit the wood. This Right of Way ends here. Retrace your steps back to Campsie Road.

Milton of Campsie to Lennoxtown

About an hour round trip

Starting from Milton Cross go south on Birdston Road over the Glazert Water and turn left down to the former station; the platforms are still in evidence. Turn right under the road and keep on the Railway Walkway, crossing the Lennoxtown-to-Torrance road (B822). At the next road, Station Road, turn right and where it meets the main road through Lennoxtown is the start of the group of Lennoxtown walks.

Community history – Don Martin

Lennoxtown

The focus of the Lennoxtown area, in former times, was the busy Lennox Mill, where tenants of the Woodhead estate brought their corn to be ground. There were several corn mills in Campsie Parish, but this was arguably the most important. Lennox Mill was located in the vicinity of the recently demolished Kali Nail Works.

A significant event in the history of the locality was the establishment, during the late 1780s, of the calico printing works at Lennoxmill, on a site adjacent to the old corn mill. Calico is a type of cotton cloth, and the printing of cotton cloth was soon established as a major industry in the area, also at Milton of Campsie. It was to provide accommodation for the block makers and other cotton printing workers that the village of Lennoxtown was established, during the late eighteenth and early nineteenth centuries. Streets of houses were planned and built according to a formal plan. Lennoxtown was at first known as "Newtown of Campsie", to distinguish it from the "Kirktown" or "Clachan" of Campsie, at the foot of Campsie Glen.

During the nineteenth century Lennoxtown grew to be the largest centre of population in Campsie Parish. Another important industry was soon established, namely a chemical works, by Charles Macintosh (of waterproof clothing fame) and his associates. At first their principal product was alum, a chemical employed in the textile industry. Alum schist, the basic ingredient in the process, was mined in the area. The works came to be known as the "Secret Works", presumably because of the need to keep the industrial processes secret.

During the 1790s many of the Lennoxmill workers supported Thomas Muir of Huntershill in his campaigns to establish democracy in Scotland, and a Reform Society was set up in Campsie in 1792. However, the parish minister, the Rev. James Lapslie, saw to it that there was also some opposition to Muir's ideas in the area. An important milestone in the drive towards democratization was the establishment of a local co-operative society, the Lennoxtown Friendly Victualling Society, one of the earliest of its kind in Scotland, in 1812.

The growing importance of Lennoxtown was underlined by the removal of the Parish Church from the Clachan to the "New Town" during the 1820s. Plans for the new church were prepared by David Hamilton, a well-known Glasgow architect. A Roman Catholic Church was erected in 1846 (originally St Paul's, later renamed St Machan's), one of the earliest post-Reformation Catholic churches in Scotland, apart from those in cities and large towns.

The decline of the industries that flourished during the nineteenth century, and also the later nail-making industry (and indeed the famous Victualling Society) has left Lennoxtown in a kind of post-industrial limbo, from which it has been difficult to escape. However, progress continues to be made, and many people have found the foothills of the Campsies at Lennoxtown an attractive location to set up home.

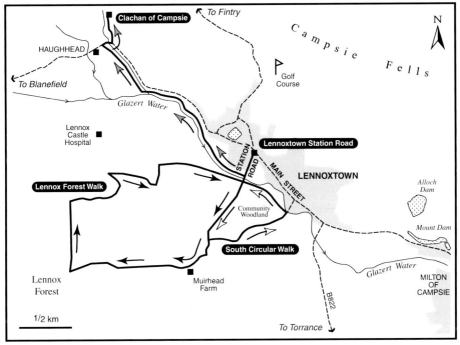

Campsie, Lennoxtown Station Road

How to get there. Walk from Milton of Campsie, as described. Bus Glasgow–
Campsie Glen.

Lennoxtown

Circular walk, about 50 minutes

Commence this walk from Station Road on the west side of Lennoxtown. Station Road
runs from the main street approximately south. There is a small car park with toilets.
Walk along Station Road in a southerly direction, over the bridge (no. 1) spanning the
Glazert Water and the old railway line. The roadside hedges are rich in various plants.
There are foxgloves, hogweed, sweet cicely, silver weed, hedge parsley and coltsfoot. If
you cross over the Glazert in the evening, you may see Daubenton's bats hawking over
the river. After a short distance the road straightens out, going uphill. At the top of the hill
the road turns gradually to the left. Shortly you will see a farm track going off to your left
downhill. From this track you get a first-class view back towards Lennoxtown and the
Campsie Fells. The Campsie Fells clearly show the banding due to approximately thirty

121

successive lava flows that formed the hills. Continue the walk down this track, to the bottom. Before reaching the bridge (no. 2), you will see a signpost showing a footpath off to your left. This path for a time runs parallel with the river and the old railway line. Follow this path till it exits on to Station Road at the bridge (no. 1), and your approximate starting point.

Lennoxtown – Forest Walk

About two and a quarter hours

This walk commences from the small car park at Station Road, which is on the west side of Lennoxtown. Walk along Station Road in a southerly direction, over the small bridge that spans the Glazert Water and the old railway track. As you walk along the hedge-lined road there are plants such as dandelion, burdock and elder, which would be of interest to the home-made wine producer. Of less interest but more attractive is bittersweet, which is a member of the deadly nightshade family. After a short distance the road straightens out, going uphill. The road turns left and then right, still going uphill, and a farm will appear on your left. Continue on the road; you are now heading in a westerly direction. Just past the farm, a sign shows a track going off to the left, heading for Torrance. Continue on the road, still heading west. When you reach a barrier, turn sharp right and enter the forest. You are now heading due north, towards the Campsie Fells.

Continue through the forest until you come to a T-junction. Take the track to your right heading east. Follow this track as it gradually goes downhill and a little to your left. The track turns into a path, and continues downhill. It shortly makes a sharper left turn and exits the forest again at a T-junction, where you take the path to the right.

Heading once again in an easterly direction, you will see some beech trees on your left. Continue on the path going slightly downhill. When you reach a small stream, cross to the other side and follow the stream downhill through the large beech trees. You will exit from the trees on to the back road to Lennox Castle Hospital. Turn right along this road, past the farm on your left; you are once again heading east. When you come to the T-junction, turn left. You are now back on Station Road, and the end of the walk.

Lennoxtown to Clachan of Campsie

About an hour

Go down Station Road and turn right on to the Railway Walkway. On the right is a large new housing estate, formerly the site of the local nail works. The only industrial activity is the distribution depot for Campsie Spring water, unfortunately marketed under the retailers' own labels and so not as widely known as it might be. The route goes through a wooded area, and under a road into the grounds of Lennox Castle Hospital, at present in the process of closing. As the Walkway nears the main road, turn left into a second entrance to the Hospital then immediately right back on to the Walkway, which now goes over the burn coming in from Clachan of Campsie to join the Glazert Water. The Walkway now goes on to its end at Strathblane, but take the right fork, which leads along the right bank of the burn to the village of Haughead. Cross the main A891 Strathblane-to-Milton of Campsie road, pass the entrance to the Schoenstatt Shrine, which will be visited later, and turn left, following the pavement to Clachan of Campsie, the start of the final walks of this part.

Community history – Don Martin

Clachan of Campsie

For centuries the Clachan of Campsie was the site of the Parish Church of Campsie. Remains of the last church to be built there can still be seen in the graveyard. The original church was erected over the reputed grave of St Machan, at the foot of the Glen, and indeed was named after that Saint. The Parish Church of Campsie was moved to Lennoxtown during the 1820s, when the High Church was built. The "St Machan" name was later given to the Roman Catholic Church in Lennoxtown, built as St Paul's in 1846.

Campsie Glen's reputation as an unrestricted place of recreation can be credited to John McFarlan (1767–1846), laird of the nearby Ballencleroch Estate. Towards the end of the eighteenth century he decided to make his side of the Glen available to the public, on a point of principle. Public access to the entire Glen was possible from 1830, when Miss Margaret Lennox of Woodhead Estate decided to follow John McFarlan's example. During the remainder of the nineteenth century the Glen grew in popularity. Guidebooks were published and many hundreds of visitors arrived each summer weekend, often in large parties accompanied by musicians.

A key attraction was the Crown Inn (now the Aldessan Gallery), which had been rebuilt by Miss Lennox in 1818 and given into the care of the renowned publican William Muir soon afterwards. Over the years there were many reports of over-exuberant behaviour on the part of visitors, so perhaps it came as no surprise when the Crown lost its licence in 1922. It was almost immediately reopened as the Red Tub Tea Rooms and run by a group of well-known local ladies, including Miss Kincaid-Lennox of Lennox Castle. In this new guise it soon became as famous as it had been as the Crown, but it closed down during World War II and did not reopen afterwards. Nowadays the building houses a tea room once again, as part of the craft shop known as the Aldessan Gallery.

Visitors to Campsie Glen should note the old parish school, which stands on the left-hand side at the approach to the Clachan, and remember the history of the Aldessan Gallery and its long-term importance to the amenity of the Glen. In the adjacent graveyard the remains of the old parish church should be noted, also the mausoleum of the Lennox family. Graves worth looking for include those of William Boick, a Covenanter, John Bell of Antermony, who was famous for his travels to Asia, and William Muir, a local poet whose poems included graphic descriptions of local life 200 years ago.

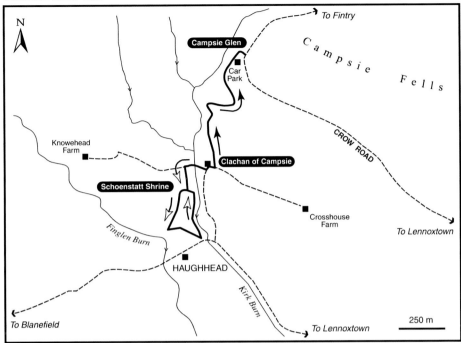

Clachan of Campsie

How to get there. Walk from Lennoxtown, as described. Bus Glasgow–Campsie Glen

Campsie Glen

About an hour

From the newly refurbished courtyard at the Clachan go alongside the row of shops and turn left up the path at the side of the buildings. At the gate, pause to read the noticeboard and admire the first of a series of wooden sculptures of animals. Further on there are benches carved from massive tree trunks. The path continues up, with the burn on the left, until a carved wooden hand forbids further progress. The path is dangerous from this point on, so a return has to be made to the gate. Now turn left and up the hill by a recently made path to the car park and view point at the bend in the Crow Road. Return by the same route.

125

Schoenstatt Shrine

Less than an hour

Facing south from the courtyard at the Clachan of Campsie, turn right into Knowhead Road, cross the burn and turn left through the ornamental gates into the grounds of Schoenstatt. On the left the former orchard is being renovated. Ballencleroch House, the purpose-built Retreat and Conference Centre, is run by a German religious order the Schoenstatt Sisters of Mary and offers a perfect setting to reflect and find peace and tranquillity. The name Schoenstatt means "beautiful place". The building is on the site of a former hotel that was burned down. Pass the Centre and cross the garden to the Shrine, a beautiful chapel, open to the public. Next go south down the avenue until just before the gates, and take the woodland walk to the left. This leads back to the Centre. Turn right, and return by your original route to the Clachan.

District and Community Council contacts

North Lanarkshire District Council, The Access Officer, Palacerigg House, Cumbernauld G67 2HU

Gartcosh Community Council
Mr Bryan Johnston
Griffin Lodge
Gartcosh G69 8AY

Stepps & District Community Council
Mr Neil Etherington
85 Whiteford Road
Stepps G33 6GA

Moodiesburn Community Council
Ms Ann Tobia
27 Edington Gardens
Moodiesburn G69 07W

Auchinloch Community Council
Ms Sarah McEwan
7 Burnbrae Road
Auchinloch

Chryston Community Council
Miss Rita Anderson
1 Neuk Avenue
Muirhead
Chryston G69 9EX

East Dunbartonshire District Council, The Access Officer, The Triangle, Bishopbriggs

Lenzie Community Council
Ms Philippa Stephenson, Secretary
27 Charles Crescent
Lenzie G66

Baldernock Community Council
Elspeth Sharkey, Secretary
The Mailings
Balmore Road
Bardowie G62 6ES

Waterside Community Council
Mrs Margaret Whiteford, Secretary
18 Gray Street
Waterside
Kirkintilloch G66 3LL

Torrance Community Council
Ms Irene McKay, Secretary
2 Craigmarloch Avenue
Torrance G64 4AY

Twechar Community Council
Ms Linda McDowell, Chair
Annfield Cottage
Twechar G65

Milton of Campsie Community Council
Ms Elizabeth McCallum, Secretary
Milton of Campsie G66

Campsie Community Council
Mrs A. Dempsey, Secretary
De Porres
98 Crosshill Street
Lennoxtown G65 2HQ

Kirkintilloch Community Council
Mrs Rhondda Geekie, Secretary
59 Iona Way
Kirkintilloch G66 3QB

Bishopbriggs Community Council
Mr Thomas Dibble, Secretary
41 Brackenbrae Road
Bishopbriggs G64 2EX

City of Glasgow District Council, The Access Officer, Provan Hall House, Easterhouse G34 9QN

Part Two

About Part Two

Having explored the neighbourhoods of Strathkelvin, you will find the walks and excursions in this part go further afield, and in general take a whole day.

When walking in the Campsies, it is advisable to be well shod for off-path walking; to be well clad for unexpected deterioration in the weather; to carry map and compass and be able to use them*; and to be with a companion or companions.

The railway walkway and the canal towpath walks are similar to the walks in Part One, only longer.

Membership of the organisations described further on (excluding Scottish Natural Heritage), is open to all, with leaders on hand to plan outings and arrange transport, where necessary.

*Ordnance Survey produce an excellent (free) leaflet *Map Reading Made Easy*, obtainable by phoning 0845 200 2717. Web site www.ordnancesurvey.co.uk

Rangers at Mugdock Country Park arrange (free) map and compass courses. Craigallion Road Nr. Milngavie, Glasgow G62 8EL. Telephone 0141 956 6100.

'Boots Across Scotland' arrange (subsidised) navigation courses. Contact Jane Kale on 0131 447 9328.

A recent publication *Navigation for Walkers* by Julian Tippett (Cordet £7.99) provides DIY training.

The four maps included are part of Ordnance Survey Landranger Map 64, 1:50 000 covering the area of former Strathkelvin District now part of East Dunbartonshire and North Lanarkshire Districts.

Overprinted are the footpaths and rights of way recognised by the Scottish Rights of Way and Access Society.

Both of these organisations have kindly granted permission for the maps to be reproduced in this book.

Walking in the Campsies

Campsie foothills

About two and a half hours

Start at Clachan of Campsie. At the bus terminus, on the right, in a garden, there is an attractive shrub called Stag's horn sumach. It is not a native species, but seems to grow extremely well. It has velvety branches, which resemble stags' antlers. In late summer it has bright red fruits, which resemble upright red tulip flowers. Go east, following the signed footpath to Lennoxtown. This is a Right of Way, the first to be taken through the courts at the instigation of local walkers and the Ramblers' Association. Do look out for barbed wire at stiles and try not to disturb cattle or sheep, especially at lambing time. Where the Right of Way finishes at Lennoxtown Park, cross the park towards the houses and climb the steps to a road between the houses. Follow this to the end and turn right, crossing the road to another flight of steps. Go down the steps, taking care, as they are often slippery, and then cross the field before climbing the hill ahead. Keep close to the fence until you reach the twin hedges, planted by the owners of the Glazert Estate to aid their workers to get to and from work.

Walk between the hedges, taking care towards the end, where the path is narrow and broken. Follow the path through the wood, eventually coming out on to a tarred road opposite stone steps that lead to old cottages.

At this point divert to the left up a steep hill to the left of the farm house. At the top cross a small burn, then turn left and walk forward to see the remains of Maidens Castle – a nice spot to picnic and enjoy the view. Return to the steps, go on downhill, turn left at the main road and follow the pavement past two large houses on the right and then some newer houses. At the first opening turn right then right again, then left and over a bridge on to the Railway Walkway. To the left, the path leads back to Kirkintilloch and Moodiesburn, but turn right and keep on the Walkway through the entrance to Lennox Castle Hospital.

After crossing the bridge over the burn where the main Walkway goes on to Strathblane, take the right fork, which follows the right bank of the burn up to Haughead. Cross the main road and enter the grounds of Schoenstatt, described in Part 1, in the Clachan of Campsie walk. Take either the nature trail to the right or the main carriage way to the house and chapel. Both lead to the back, another gate and a quiet road. Turn right, over the burn and then left, back to the bus terminus.

Campsie skyline
About two and a half hours

Starting at the Clachan of Campsie, join the path behind the cottages and follow the zigzag path to the bend in the Crow Road. On the Kirk Burn you may see dipper, grey wagtail and pied wagtail. As you climb up the path away from the burn, wheatear, meadow pipit and curlew are to be seen. Cross the road and walk up the shoulder of the hill until you reach a path at the top. Walking along the path you will pass a stone cairn on the left, and from this you can see the next cairn. Follow the path to the second cairn.

The path will then veer to the right, down a dip and across a stile. The path then goes up and passes another small cairn situated on the path. To the right of this you will see another cairn close to the edge of the Campsies. Walk over to this cairn.

Go downhill, slightly to the right, until you meet a fence with a gate. This takes you to the waterworks for "Campsie Spring Water". Follow the wide path here, down to a burn. Cross the burn and go through the gate in the wall. Now cross a field with a burn on the left and go through another gate at the bottom that leads to a stony path at the right of a farmhouse.

An interesting extra here is to walk over the grass to the right, then straight forward – you will be walking on the remains of Maidens Castle.

Continue down the path, passing a farmhouse away to the left. Follow the track for a few hundred yards, passing a cottage on the right where a small woodland begins. Continue down the track until you arrive at a few stone steps on your left. Turn right here, through the woodland, following a path that veers slightly to the right and joins a path in the clearing after leaving the wood. Keeping the fence on your right and the burn on your left, walk along here until you reach the "twin hedges". Walk between the hedges, leaving them at a gate at the end.

Veer slightly right and go over the hill ahead, following the fence on the right. Climb the flight of stairs up to the houses. Turn right then left, following between the houses until you reach a few steps down to a playing field. You are now following the Right of Way. Cross straight over, at the side of the building, until you reach a path. Turn right, then left, following this path until you reach a road, the Crow Road.

Cross over, bearing right, then left, to meet a path and stile. From here walk to the fence/wall facing where you will find another stile. (There is no path on this field, which can be very wet, and it is usually best to keep to the left of the reedy area.) Turn sharp left, then right, between the old farm buildings to join the path between trees. At the end of this track turn right, and then over the stile, to arrive beside a house.

Walk on the path behind the house, cross the stile where it is often very muddy, and keep walking next to the wall on your left until you find a high stile into the next field. Cross over, turn right and, after a few minutes, cross the next stile straight ahead.

From here cross the field to the gate and the stony track, and keep walking along the foothill on the Right of Way until you reach Clachan of Campsie. Please remember to close all the farm gates behind you and do not disturb the sheep and lambs, especially during lambing time.

131

Lecket Hill

About two and a half hours

From Clachan of Campsie, after leaving the cottages to the left, follow the path up to the bend in the Crow Road. Before you leave the glen take the opportunity to examine the geology of the area. The Kirk Burn has cut through the various layers of the rock formation. There is a sequence of limestones, shales and lava flows, for which the Campsie Fells are famous. Keep on the recently made path to the left of the road with the steep slopes of Campsie Glen to the left, passing Jamie Wright's Well on the other side of the road. Where the path ends, take to the road, where two burns join, one coming alongside the road and the other down from the glen on the right, to go under the road (GR 625808). Just after this point, take the well-defined path on the right uphill, leading to the top of Lecket Hill (GR 645812, 546 metres). After enjoying the views, leave the top in a south-easterly direction on fairly flat ground and then go uphill to the Cort-ma-Law trig point (GR 652 799, 531 metres). On the higher ground you may see a peregrine falcon, a kestrel, a buzzard and, if you are fortunate, a short-eared owl or a hen harrier. The last two species are more difficult to see now, due to unsympathetic land management. Meadow pipits abound, carrion crow and raven occur and the attractive golden plover may be seen. Now go south-west over the next hill (Lair's Hill, GR 640798, 504 metres) and keep going in a westerly direction past two more cairns and down to the bend in the road. Cross over and take the path down to the Clachan of Campsie.

Meikle Bin

About five hours

Start from the Clachan of Campsie. The woodland in the glen supports a varied bird population including chaffinch, robin, wren, spotted flycatcher, blackcap and chiffchaff. After looking at the bird life, go up to the bend in the road; carry on up the road to the top of Lecket Hill as previously described. On reaching the stiles at the fence junction, GR 638812, cross the right-hand stile and follow the narrow path to the summit cairn, GR 645812, 546 metres. Go north to the fence, climb over and follow it down in an easterly direction almost to the Bin Burn, to the break in the trees on the left. Go through the break (roughish going) then down the second break on the right, to pass the end of the forest road. Continue north-east down to and across the Bin Burn, then ascend to the left of the fence to another forest road (a steepish climb).

On the moor there is a good population of short-tailed field voles and the water vole also occurs, although it has a problem avoiding the mink, which are also in the area. Roe deer, hare and rabbit are also found. The path to the summit trig point of Meikle Bin, GR 668822, 570 metres, starts at a small cairn across this road – a relatively easy ascent. Return by the same path to the forest road, although a descent west towards the trees will allow a viewing of parts of a plane thought to have crashed during the war. If this is done, head north from the wreckage to meet the main descent path. Continue down by the outward route to recross the Bin Burn and ascend to the forest road. Turn right initially north-west, becoming west then south-west, back to the Crow Road Cross, to face the oncoming traffic back to Clachan of Campsie.

Holehead

About three hours

From the Clachan of Campsie go up as for Lecket Hill, but instead of leaving the road to climb it, keep on to the former Regional boundary between East Dunbartonshire and Stirling District, GR 630820. On the left of the road a wall goes off at right angles uphill, in a north-westerly direction. This is the boundary. Follow it, keeping the wall on the right. Before it bends to the left, heading west, look out for the trig pillar over to the left. It may be difficult to spot if there is low cloud (and there often is), so keep on until the wall bends slightly to the right. At this point head due south for the trig pillar, GR 618827, 551 metres. On it, it has a plaque: Strathkelvin Ramblers 1992. The story of the adoption of the pillar from Ordnance Survey is told in the publication *The First Five Years*, obtainable from any member of the Strathkelvin Group.

This is a walk where skylark and meadow pipit are common as well as red grouse. If you are fortunate, you may see its rarer cousin, the black grouse, and if you venture over to the conifers the crossbill is a possibility. Return by the same route.

Note The Ordnance Survey, a few years ago, announced that they now surveyed by satellite. Their well known landmarks, the triangulation pillars, or trig points as they are commonly known, would therefore be redundant. Rather than have these deteriorate into unsightly ruins, applications were invited from people willing to adopt one. Strathkelvin Ramblers applied and were sent a complete list of all pillars in OS Landranger 64 Glasgow and Surrounding Area. Bar Hill (709 762, 155 metres) was the nearest, lowest and most interesting, because it is on the Antonine Wall near a well restored Roman Fort. However, this had already been adopted by Historic Scotland. Holehead (618 827, 551 metres) in the Campsies was chosen. This was granted, subject to the permission of the landowner. Finding who that was proved to be difficult. Apparently there is no readily available record until someone applies for planning permission. Eventually he was located and readily gave consent. Since then, the Group has climbed there on several occasions by varied routes. The pillar has also been visited each year by a small working party to repair, repaint and fix a plaque: "Strathkelvin Ramblers 1992".

To adopt a pillar, write to Adopt-a-Trig Pillar, Ordnance Survey, Romsay Road, Maybush, Southampton, Hants SO9 4DH, stating the area in which you are interested.

Clachan of Campsie to Spout of Ballagan

Allow three hours to do justice to the geology and flora of the area

Leave the bus terminus at the Clachan and go down to Haughead either by the road or through Schoenstatt. Cross the road and go through a gap in the buildings to join a spur of the Railway Walkway. Continue until you reach the junction with the main path. Turn right and keep on the path until it ends at the main road (A891) opposite the church at Strathblane. Turn right, back towards Clachan of Campsie, and shortly you come to a gateway on the left of Ballagan House. Turn in and go along the drive, keeping the main house and outhouses to the right. Ballagan Glen is a Scottish Wildlife Trust Reserve and is situated on private property. Because there is no path up the Glen, anyone wishing to gain access by this difficult route should first contact the Scottish Wildlife Trust, 71 Houldsworth Street, Glasgow G3 (telephone 0141 248 4647).

The alternative access to view the Spout of Ballagan is by leaving the Railway Walkway a bit before it ends, on a track to the right (north), clearly leading to Ballagan Farm. Cross the road. Take the farm track towards the farmhouse, going through the gate on the left before reaching the house. The farmer has no objection to walkers using this path. As it zigzags uphill, at a point where it seems to be going too far to the right, leave it and go to the left. On the 350 metre contour line (GR 580 803),a faint track is soon picked up, leading to the top of the waterfall (GR 573 802).

From this position we get an excellent view into Ballagan Glen, which is formed by the Ballagan Burn cascading down a series of waterfalls. The top waterfall is the impressive Spout of Ballagan. The layers of rock that are exposed are the Ballagan Beds, composed of layers of cement stones and shales. At the top of the cliff there is sandstone with overlying basaltic lavas. The beds were laid down about 340 million years ago during the Carboniferous Era, when the area was subject to river and lagoon action.

In the glen, due to a basic flush condition, there is a surprising variety of plants, which number in the order of 200 species. Because of the variety of habitats there is a large invertebrate population by the burn, which in turn supports dipper, grey wagtail and heron. In the woodland, tits, robins, thrushes, buzzards, sparrowhawks and green woodpeckers are to be found, and in summer willow and wood warblers, spotted flycatchers and cuckoos.

Return by the same route.

Earl's Seat via Fin Glen
About five hours

From Clachan of Campsie walk back south towards the main Strathblane road and turn right through Haughead to the lane on the right, signposted for the Morris Furniture factory. Proceed up the lane to the factory and veer left on to the farm track, through a gate and on, parallel to the Finglen Burn on your right, up to a ruined farmhouse. This is a good area to look for the mountain pansy, which occurs in both yellow and blue-violet forms. Continue up the path through a second gate, aiming for a cairn visible on a ridge ahead to the right of a line of trees.

Beyond the cairn, follow the clear path north-west through bracken to a wall surmounted by a fence. Here view the waterfalls across Fin Glen on the Almeel Burn. Cross the wall and fence at the right side of the obvious two tall posts – no barbed wire at this point! (Care is required, as getting over here is really quite awkward, but there is no gate or better place to cross in the vicinity.)

Ascend the field still heading north-west towards the fence on the skyline and follow the fence to where it turns sharp left. Here, leave the fence to avoid the worst of the rough and boggy ground but continue to walk parallel to it, heading roughly west. Remain with the fence as it turns increasingly to the north, first of all to the summit of Dumbreck, GR 574 815, 508 metres, TP) and on undulating to Earl's Seat (GR 570 839, 578 metres, TP).

The mountain hare, which turns white in winter to merge with the snow covering, is fairly common in this area. Unfortunately, the hare does not seem to know when it is not sitting on snow. This means that you can walk up to a bright white hare sitting on blackish peat.

Return by the same route. About two and a half to three hours, excluding stops.

There is an alternative route, involving a short stretch of roadway, or a bus if available. Go along the Railway Walkway to its end at the A803 opposite the church. Turn left, go down to the main A81, turn right at the Kirkhouse Inn and go through the village to the War Memorial. Take the right fork along a road between houses on the right and a bowling club on the left. This is the route of the water main from Loch Katrine to Milngavie. Keep on the road, past the end of the houses, through a succession of gates to Cantiwherry Cottage, GR 545 814. At a bend in the road to the left, take the path uphill to the right, keeping to the right of the woodland. Head for the coll between Dumgoyne, GR 541828, 427 metres, and the hill to its right, GR 547 825. If desired, go to the top of Dumgoyne – a short steep ascent by any route. The best plan is probably to skirt round anticlockwise and go up from the north-west. Now follow the well defined path in a north-easterly direction up to Garloch Hill, GR 553 834, 543 metres. Now veer to the right in a north-east by easterly direction, avoiding the steep slope down to the left, and go on to the top of Earl's Seat, GR 570 838, 578 metres, on the District boundary.

Return by the same route, or straight down past Dumgoyne in the direction of the distillery to the road over the pipeline, turning left to the War Memorial.

Strathkelvin railway walkway

Having walked from Gartcosh in the south to Clachan of Campsie in the north, exploring each Community Council area in turn, and having spent some time climbing in the Campsie Fells, you can now return south directly by the walkway.

The railway route

Strathkelvin railway walkway stretches for 13 miles, through rural towns and quiet villages, out into open countryside with breathtaking views of the Campsie Fells. Running from Strathblane in the north, past Lennox Castle and through the heart of Kirkintilloch and Lenzie, the walk continues to Moodiesburn in the south.

Designed to accommodate the needs of all walkers, the walkway for the most part consists of a level, well surfaced path with few major roads to cross. Much of the path is suitable for prams, pushchairs and wheelchairs and is ideal for cyclists.

Waymarks displaying a steam engine point the way along the railway walkway. Users of the path can pause to enjoy the peace and quiet of the countryside, or may take a short detour into Kirkintilloch town centre. Whatever your interest and no matter how far you walk or cycle along the path, you are sure to enjoy your visit to the railway walkway.

Railway history

Strathkelvin railway walkway follows the route of the former Monkland and Kirkintilloch Railway, the Edinburgh and Glasgow (Campsie Branch) Railway and the Blane Valley Railway.

Opened in 1826, the Monkland and Kirkintilloch Railway linked the coalfields of Monklands with the Forth and Clyde Canal at Kirkintilloch, enabling the transportation of coal to the Lothians and Clydeside. The railway was taken out of service in 1965–66.

The Edinburgh and Glasgow (Campsie Branch) Railway opened in 1848, leaving the main line at Lenzie to continue northwards to Milton of Campsie and Lennoxtown. In 1866 an extension was opened through the Blane Valley to Killearn and later to Aberfoyle. This route was closed to passengers beyond Kirkintilloch in 1951 and between Lenzie and Kirkintilloch in 1964. Closure to goods was in 1966.

Flora and fauna

Nearly all the route is on the line of the disused railway, which sounds rather uninteresting. However, the slag infill to the embankment gives a well-drained foundation, which tends to be base rich. Where the lineside drainage is disrupted, marshy areas develop, giving considerable variation in habitat. As a result, in the spring the wet areas can be brightened with golden saxifrage and marsh marigold, while the drier areas are rich with flowers including herb-Robert and speedwells. The trees and shrubs along the walkway vary from oak, sycamore, ash and hazel to hawthorn, gorse and broom.

As you would expect, the bird life varies depending on the locality. Buzzard and kestrel are fairly common and, if you are fortunate, the sparrow hawk and peregrine may appear. The peregrine is more likely to be seen in the proximity of the Campsies. Along the hedge and shrub areas, chaffinch, dunnock, robin, crows, magpies and blue, great, coal and long-tailed tits are fairly common. As you approach the housing areas, house sparrows should also be seen. This is a declining species and in years to come may become a rarity. Where the route is adjacent to the Glazert Water of the Bothlin Burn and where SEPA, the environmental agency, are successful in ensuring unpolluted water rich in aquatic insects, you should see the dipper, kingfisher and grey and pied wagtails.

District boundary to Southbrae, Lennoxtown

Starting from Strathblane in East Dunbartonshire, walkers soon reach Strathkelvin, where the railway walkway skirts the foot of the Campsie Fells before running in to the cool shade of Lennox Forest with its splendid castle. From here the walkway follows the course of the Glazert Water, passing a picturesque weir and, in just under a mile, reaches Lennoxtown.

There are access points at Strathblane Road, Strathblane, Lennox Castle Hospital (main goods entrance) and South Brae, Lennoxtown. There is a bus terminus at Clachan of Campsie.

Southbrae, Lennoxtown to Milton of Campsie

The railway walkway skirts the southern edge of Lennoxtown, which itself offers all the usual amenities and services of a small town. The walkway continues through parkland, crossing Staneybrae beside the Glazertbank Hotel and onwards to Rowantree Terrace east of Lennoxtown. Milton of Campsie is soon reached and a new link path provides access at the residential area at Valleyfield. The walkway passes under Birdston Road, near Milton of Campsie village cross, where the railway station was situated (original platforms have been restored) and continues through the public park.

There are access points at Staneybrae, Lennoxtown (adjacent to the Glazertbank Hotel); Rowantree Terrace, Lennoxtown; Valleyfield, Milton of Campsie; and Birdston Road, Milton of Campsie (public park).

Milton of Campsie to Kilsyth Road, Kirkintilloch

Continuing through the public park, the walkway turns southwards to rejoin the course of the Glazert Water and follows this until it meets the River Kelvin, which is spanned by a new footbridge. At Birdston junction you can still see the viaduct that carried the Kelvin Valley Railway over the Campsie Branch Railway and the Glazert Water. The railway walkway continues southwards, descending a flight of shallow steps to reach Kilsyth Road, where there are various routes through Kirkintilloch town centre – either by the Cowgate with its shops and amenities or through the Luggie Water Park, where an aqueduct carries the Forth and Clyde Canal and towpath across the railway walkway.

There are access points at Birdston Road, Birdston (link path to walkway); the industrial estate, Birdston Road; Kilsyth Road, Kirkintilloch (flight of steps); and Luggie Water Park, Kirkintilloch.

Industry Street, Kirkintilloch to Woodilee Road, Lenzie

Following through Luggie Water Park, the railway walkway reaches Townhead via a new subway under the relief road. From Industry Street, the walkway continues through Woodhead Park to the rear of the Community Centre and onwards towards Woodilee. Alternatively, walkers can proceed via Lenzie Road to join the walkway at Whitegates, opposite the District Council headquarters. After a short distance, the path crosses Woodilee Road, adjacent to Woodilee Hospital, before continuing southwards.

There are access points at Industry Street, Kirkintilloch; Whitegates, Lenzie Road, Kirkintilloch (opposite Strathkelvin District Council Offices); and Woodilee Road, Lenzie (1 mile east of Lenzie Station).

Woodilee Road, Lenzie to Gartferry Road, Bridgend

From Woodilee Road, the railway walkway swings southeastwards underneath the viaduct carrying the main Edinburgh–Glasgow railway over the disused railway and a small burn. Skirting the eastern edge of South Lenzie, the walkway follows the course of the Bothlin Burn past Claddens to Burnbrae Road. A short section of path at Burnbrae Road is not suitable for prams or wheelchairs. The walkway continues through Burnbrae Community Woodlands and over the Bothlin Burn before proceeding past the former Auchengeich Colliery at Bridgend.

There are access points at Lindsaybeg Road, Claddens (short access track); Burnbrae Road; and Gartferry Road, Bridgend (car parking available).

Gartferry Road, Bridgend to Avenuehead Road, Moodiesburn

After crossing Gartferry Road, follow the walkway past the pigeon lofts to enter Moodiesburn Glen, which is an important local wildlife area and ancient woodland, adjacent to Bothlin Burn. After weaving through the glen, the path cuts underneath the main Glasgow–Cumbernauld road, under a bridge, and curves eastwards passing Bedlay Cemetery. The railway walkway leads to Avenuehead Road where it ends, although careful walkers can continue onwards towards Coatbridge.

There are access points at Avenuehead Road, Moodiesburn; and by path from the main A80.

The River, the Wall and the Canal

The River

It is usually thought that the River Kelvin rises in the Kilsyth Hills near the village of Kelvinhead. Perhaps it did so at one time. In recent history, according to the Forth and Clyde Handbook, the source is south and east of Kelvinhead near Wyndford Lock on the canal. When the canal was being constructed, the marshy ground of Dullater Bog created difficulties. The bog had to be drained by a channel to the north side of the canal, thus forming the head waters of the River Kelvin. This accounts for the unnaturally straight course of the river alongside the canal here. The towpath and retaining bank had their foundations sunk to a depth of 50 feet to reach firm ground. The water in the bog rises to its own level to the south, offside of the canal, which accounts for the extra width of the canal at this stretch.

Part of the riverbank is visited in one of the Twechar walks; another in the walk from Bishopbriggs to Torrance. East Dunbartonshire Council has plans and has made a start on a new walkway from Birdston on the B757 between Kirkintilloch and Milton of Campsie to Milngavie, which will provide a route from Strathkelvin to the Clyde, Kelvin and Allander Walkway, in reverse.

At present the easiest connection is by the canal towpath at Kirkintilloch to the splendid aqueduct over the Kelvin at Maryhill, and downstream to the River Clyde, then upstream on the Clyde walkway to Glasgow city centre, returning to Strathkelvin by public transport. Alternatively, you may go back upstream on the Kelvin bank to the confluence of the Allander Water with the River Kelvin, staying with the Allander to Milngavie railway station.

The confluence of the Allander and Kelvin can also be reached from Strathkelvin by the A807 from Torrance, Balmore or Bardowie to the Allander Toll. From there the Allander may be reached from the A879 downstream to the confluence of the Kelvin and Allander, continuing downstream alongside the Kelvin to the Clyde, or from the B8049 upstream to Milngavie railway station. There is public transport from either destination back to Strathkelvin.

The Antonine Wall

History

Hadrian's Wall was the frontier system designed to secure occupied Britain against hostile penetration from the north by checking all movement across the 75 miles of country between the River Tyne and the Solway Firth. North Britons continued to exert pressure against Roman garrisons, and so when Hadrian was succeeded by Antoninus Pius the lowlands were subdued and occupied and another wall was constructed.

The Antonine Wall, which was completed in AD 142 or 143, extended for 35 miles from the Firth of Forth to the River Clyde to form a barrier across the narrowest part of Britain. The defences comprised essentially a ditch, generally about 40 feet wide and 12 feet deep, backed by a rampart built for the most part of turf blocks set upon a stone foundation about 14 feet broad. The garrison occupied forts that were attached to the rear of the rampart and were linked by a military road.

Soon after its completion the military situation further south necessitated the evacuation of the wall. Before long, the wall was overwhelmed by attacks from the north. The wall was finally abandoned shortly before the end of the 2nd century. Further information may be obtained by visiting the Hunterian Museum in the University of Glasgow, and the public libraries in Kirkintilloch and Falkirk.

Present day
Parts of the wall may be conveniently explored from several of the walks in Part 1, particularly Bishopbriggs, Kirkintilloch and Twechar. Others further afield are described in the chapter on the Forth and Clyde Canal, from Bowling in the west to Falkirk in the east.

The Antonine Walkway Trust describes a walk near Croy: Craigmarloch to Croy, Twechar, 5–6 miles; around the network, 2–4 miles; Croy station to Craigmarloch, 2 miles; Croy station to Twechar, 5–6 miles. For further information, contact John McColl (Secretary), 24 Cuilmuir Terrace, Croy, Kilsyth G65 9HR.

The Canals and the Millennium Link - Guthrie Hutton
The Forth and Clyde Canal runs between Grangemouth and Bowling. It is joined at Falkirk by the Edinburgh and Glasgow Union Canal – better known as simply the Union Canal. The two form one of central Scotland's prime environmental and recreational resources, and yet they came close to being ruined in the 1960s and 1970s.

The Forth and Clyde is the older, being constructed – or "cut", as the making of a canal is more properly described – in two phases. The first, between 1768 and 1777, took it from Grangemouth to Glasgow, and was completed from Glasgow to Bowling between 1785 and 1790. The main Glasgow terminal at Port Dundas was also created around 1790. Plans to make a canal from Edinburgh to the west were thwarted by the Napoleonic wars, and so it was not until 1818 that work began on the Union Canal. It was completed in 1822. The two canals therefore came from either end of the great canal-building boom and represent a fascinating contrast in engineering techniques. They also differ in that the Forth and Clyde was capable of taking sea-going vessels, while the Union was purely an inland barge canal.

Completion of the Edinburgh and Glasgow Railway in 1842 saw trade collapse on the Union. Before the decade was out, the railway company had bought the failing canal but was bound by Act of Parliament to maintain it, and so the canal survived. The Forth and Clyde continued to prosper until closure of the Forth Ports during the First World War forced trade onto the railways. It never returned and a long, steady decline led to closure on 1 January 1963. The Union was closed in 1965. For 10 years or more, an orgy of culverting and infilling chopped the canals into isolated ponds, but despite the damage they remained largely intact.

Through the 1970s and 1980s, campaigning groups such as the Forth and Clyde Canal Society set about raising the profile of the canals and the authorities began to take notice. The culverting stopped and gradual improvements began to be made. Towpaths were remade, bridges rebuilt and lock gates replaced. The slow but steady pace was replaced in the mid-1990s by the launch of the Millennium Link Project. Its approval in 1998 brought in large sums of money to restore the two canals to full navigation and thereby provide a catalyst for the regeneration of the canal corridor through central Scotland.

The centrepiece of the restoration scheme is the new link between the canals, to the west of Falkirk. This was needed because the original link, a flight of 11 locks, was removed in 1933. New buildings, roads and other developments have made the line of the old locks unusable and so a new site for the junction between the canals has been selected. To reach it the Union Canal has been extended for about a mile along the south side of the railway, to the west of Falkirk High station. At the end of this extension it drops through two conventional locks into a huge new basin. There it turns through 90° and heads for a new tunnel under the railway and the Antonine Wall. As you emerge from the tunnel the view to the north over Larbert to the Ochil Hills is spectacular, although a boater negotiating the canal will have little time to admire it. The canal is now on an aqueduct that leads to the world's only rotating boat-lift – the Falkirk Wheel. This remarkable complex, incorporating all the major elements of canal construction, and a visitors' centre, has surely made Falkirk a required destination for canal tourists from all over the world.

There is of course much more to the Millennium Link scheme than the Falkirk Wheel. Numerous bridges have been rebuilt to replace the culverts of the 1960s and 1970s. Principal among these are the A80 crossing at Castlecary and the M8 near Broxburn. At Dalmuir, a drop-lock, another unique structure, has been built to take the canal under Dumbarton Road. A new section of canal has been created to rejoin the Forth and Clyde to the River Carron at Grangemouth, where the canal was filled-in in the late 1960s. Another new section of canal has been created through Wester Hailes on the western edge of Edinburgh, where about a mile of the Union Canal has been culverted. Also, locks have been rebuilt and regated, stonework on bridges and aqueducts has been repointed and repaired, and towpaths have been improved and the channels dredged. The canals are alive again.

Mavis Valley to Twechar

The canal through the former Strathkelvin District ran east from the old mining village of Mavis Valley to another mining community, Twechar. In 1913 an underground fire at Cadder No. 15 pit, close to Mavis Valley, killed 22 men. It was one of Scotland's worst pit disasters. There is little now remaining of the coal industry, although the rotten stumps of a railway bridge that linked the colliery to the railway network can still be seen. To the north of the canal here are the Wilderness Woods.

The bridge beside Bishopbriggs Leisuredrome has been rebuilt as part of the Millennium Link project. It was known in the canal's working days as Farm Bridge, although these days people tend to call if after Balmuildy Road or Bishopbriggs itself. There are paths on both sides of the canal between Farm and Cadder Bridges. There is a spillway on the towpath side, west of Cadder. This lets excess water escape from the canal into the adjacent burn and is part of the water-control system that keeps the canal at its proper level.

Cadder is a delightful spot with the old mill house on the towpath side and the canal cottages on the offside. Mature trees give the little village a sense of seclusion, much favoured by passengers on the pleasure steamers that plied the canal between the 1890s and 1939. Steamer passengers were always welcome at Cadder, but the church, set back from the canal, has had some unwelcome visitors too. A watchman's hut and an iron mort-safe are reminders that body snatchers, raiding from canal boats, once took an unhealthy interest in the graveyard. The sharp bend in the canal after the church is where the canal cut through the Antonine Wall. The steep bank, after the bend on the offside, is a remnant of the wall. Behind it was a Roman fort. Distant views of the Campsie Fells, from the elevated, wooded towpath embankment, add to some of the finest scenery the canal has to offer.

The original Hungryside Bridge, which carries the road to Torrance, was replaced in the 1930s by a large steel lifting bridge. The canal passes through farmland from here to the Glasgow Road Bridge, where the Stables pub/ restaurant has been created in a former canal stables, or "horse barracks" as such buildings were known. A slipway was provided on the offside here in the 1980s to cater for a growing number of large boats. The boats were based to the west of the bridge because it had been replaced by a restricted culvert, which was itself replaced by the existing bridge in the late 1980s as part of a restoration scheme known as the Glasgow Canal Project.

There is another spillway at the Park Burn on the western edge of Kirkintilloch. Closer to the town, on the offside, is a slipway where those idiosyncratic canal and coasting vessels known as puffers were repaired. Beside it was the entrance to a large canal basin where one of Scotland's earliest railways, the Monkland and Kirkintilloch, terminated. The bed of the old railway now forms part of a walkway. The small arched culvert, adjacent to the slipway, is the outfall of a canal feeder from the Bothlin Burn. It runs beside the line of the old railway for part of its route.

The sloping ground on the offside between the Seagull Trust boathouse and Townhead Bridge was the unlikely building berth of many puffers. Townhead Bridge was rebuilt as part of the Millennium Link Project with a new deck being placed on the abutments of a swing bridge built in the 1930s. Beside the bridge on the towpath side is a building that was once a hostelry known as the Eagle Inn. It dates from the time when horse-drawn passenger boats plied the canal and was later used as a temperance hotel in the days before Kirkintilloch famously became a "dry" town.

Nicolson Bridge, to the east of Townhead Bridge, carries the bypass road over the canal. Immediately to its east is the Luggie Aqueduct. This is a remarkable structure, erected about 1773 by the Falkirk contractors Gibb and Moir. Nothing like it had been built in Scotland before, and it is a true milestone of Scottish civil-engineering history. About 100 years after it was built, the Campsie Branch railway line was laid underneath it, giving the arch a somewhat truncated appearance. Access to the Railway Walkway can be had from beside the aqueduct.

Hillhead Basin, or Kirkintilloch Harbour, was Scotland's first inland port and the western terminal for the canal when it was opened to here from Grangemouth in 1773. Hillhead swing bridge was built in the 1930s and, although it lay fixed through the years when the canal was closed, it has been restored to use. Heading east out of Kirkintilloch, the canal crosses Auchendavy aqueduct. Beyond it, beside the towpath at Shirva Dyke, is another remnant of the Antonine Wall. The little mining hamlet of Tintock is opposite, and further east on the offside are the remains of St Flannan's pit, which had some of the deepest shafts in Scotland.

Across from the colliery site, on the towpath side, is the ruined Shirva stables. To the east is Shirva Pend, a remarkable aqueduct with burn, cart track and footpath running through it. There are steps down to it from the towpath. The canal straightens out as it heads for Twechar. The coal industry virtually created the village and has left its mark all around. The remains of a railway swing bridge, which linked collieries on the north side of the canal to the south can still be seen to the west of the present-day road bridge. Twechar No. 1 Pit was on the towpath side to the east of the bridge, on the other side of the canal-side road. Old pit bings on the offside to the east of the bridge clad the lower slopes of Bar Hill.

Twechar's other claim to fame is of course the Antonine Wall, which runs across Bar Hill. A Roman fort has been laid out on the hill for visitors to view. The canal skirts the base of Bar Hill as it heads east from Twechar. The wooded slopes make this a very attractive stretch of water, although those afloat have to concentrate going round the very sharp bend at Strone Point, better known to canal folk as the Devil's Elbow. The old district boundary is just around the next bend.

Beyond Strathkelvin – west

Kirkintilloch marks the centre point of the Forth and Clyde Canal between east and west, although, including the Union Canal, there is a lot more canal to the east. The towpaths offer excellent traffic-free walking from one side of the country to the other, and also links to other long-distance paths. Going west, beyond the old district boundary at Mavis Valley, the canal heads on into Glasgow past Possil Loch – a Site of Special Scientific Interest and a source of water for the canal. The character changes from countryside to urban surroundings at Lambhill. Beyond it, at Stockingfield Junction, the towpath comes to an end and has to be regained by going under the Lochburn Road aqueduct (there are plans to erect a footbridge across the canal so that may exist by the time you read this!).

East from Stockingfield is the Glasgow branch to Port Dundas. Bridges at Ruchill Street and Firhill Road were rebuilt as part of the Glasgow Canal Project in the late 1980s. Charles Rennie Mackintosh's Ruchill Church Hall is adjacent to Ruchill Street Bridge, and his Queen's Cross Church is close to Firhill Road Bridge. Partick Thistle FC's ground is alongside Firhill Road Bridge, as is the extensive Firhill Basin. British Waterways headquarters is beside the original Glasgow terminal basin at Hamilton Hill and across Possil Road is Spier's Wharf, where some very fine 19th century sugar refinery and grain mill buildings have been restored and converted into flats. At the end is a small, elegant Georgian building once used as the Canal Company's offices. The views of the city from Spier's Wharf are splendid.

West from Stockingfield the main line of the canal heads down past the Maryhill Locks and Kelvin Dock dry dock, and the magnificent Kelvin Aqueduct. The West Highland Way goes under the aqueduct and a path leads down to it. Past Govan Cottage Bridge at Cleveden Road is Temple, where two canalside pubs vie for the passing trade. Round the corner at Westerton, the canal re-enters East Dunbartonshire for a short distance. Here too is perhaps the closest railway station to the canal. Cloberhill and Blairdardie Locks take the canal down to the Great Western Road. There was a lot of reconstruction work here, associated with the Millennium Link. The Boghouse Locks continue the descent to Duntreath Avenue Bridge and Clydebank, where there was also a lot of Millennium Link reconstruction, some to accommodate the fish-and-chip boat, the Debra Rose. Beyond it the canal goes through Dalmuir, with its unique drop-lock, and on past Old Kilpatrick to Bowling.

Bishopbriggs to Ruchill Park

Starting at the Leisuredrome turn left, cross Farm Bridge and turn left again along the main towpath to Possil Loch. Go on to Lambhill Bridge, with one of the best preserved but not yet restored stable blocks on the right bank. Soon you see some new houses that have been built very close to the offside bank. The land above this, formerly Ruchill Golf Course, is being developed.

Next is Stockingfield Junction. There is a movable barrier across the canal just before the junction, thought to have been built to seal off the canal as a precaution against flooding of the city in the event of enemy action in the last war. At this point the main canal bends to the right and the Glasgow branch goes off to the left. To continue on either towpath it is necessary to go down to Lochburn Road, and then go under the main canal and turn left up a path to join the towpath now on the offside. Turning left leads on to Bowling; turning right leads along the Glasgow branch to Spiers Wharf. Here the canal appears to end, but in fact is culverted and appears again with still remaining basins and connections to the Monkland Canal, now followed by the M8 for some miles. Leave the canal at Ruchill Street Bridge, and 700 yards from Stockingfield, turn left uphill and into Ruchill Park. Keep on up, bearing left up to the flagpole, the second highest point in Glasgow, affording, on a clear day, splendid views all round. The highest point, in Springburn Park, has its views partly obscured by highrise flats.

There are now three options. First, return by the same route to Bishopbriggs (about four hours' round trip). Second, continue on the towpath to the end of the canal. Cross Craighall Street, turn left along North Canal Bank Street. Opposite the distillery entrance, cross the canal at the bascule bridge near the disused railway swing bridge. Turn left then right and alongside the canal basin and, where it opens up to the left, go uphill through Sighthill Park to the standing stones. Now cross the motorway by the footbridge, and by Kyle Street and North Hanover Street reach Buchanan Street bus station or Queen Street railway station for transport back to Bishopbriggs (about six hours' round trip). Third, continue to explore the main canal, having come so far. There are opportunities for return transport at several points, as railways follow or cross the route of the canal. Detailed plans may be made by consulting the *Forth and Clyde Handbook*.

Auchinstarry, to the south of Kilsyth, was another mining village, but also the site of a large quarry, now used by climbers to practise on. Croy Hill dominates the view to the east of the canal bridge. Its north face is clothed in pit waste from Nethercroy Colliery, but the hill can also boast a fine remnant of the Antonine Wall which, taken with the canal and Bar Hill, makes a fine circular walk. The bridge at Craigmarloch was where the canal pleasure steamers used to terminate beside a bungalow tearoom. The main canal water supply from Townhead Reservoir comes into the canal here. Alongside the lade, but set back from the canal, is another old stables building. To the east the canal crosses the Dullatur Bog as it heads for Wyndford Lock and the long descent to the east coast. The A80 at Castlecary, now rebridged by the Millennium Link, was the first blockage to close the canal. Its reopening has huge symbolic significance for canal enthusiasts.

Three locks take the canal down from Castlecary to Bonnybridge. Underwood Lockhouse, beside Lock 17, has been restored as a pub/restaurant serving Indian cuisine. A new lifting bridge has been installed at Bonnybridge, a town once dominated by the brick and light iron casting industries. On the edge of Camelon is Carmuirs railway aqueduct and just beyond it on the offside is the Falkirk Wheel, the jewel in the Millennium Link's crown. At Lock 16, where the Union Canal used to join the Forth and Clyde, is the Union Inn, a hostelry that once was beside a large basin known as Port Downie. It is one of a number of pub/restaurants through Falkirk.

The restoration of the culverted bridges and lock flight from Lock 16 through Camelon and Bainsford is another crowning achievement of the Millennium Link. Below Bainsford is Lock 4, where the canal has been reinstated through a road which has itself been replaced by the new Falkirk distributor road. Beyond it, the new "Carron Cut" takes the canal across the flat carse lands to the new Sea Lock on the River Carron.

The Ramblers' Association

The Ramblers' Association exists to facilitate, for the benefit of everyone, the enjoyment, discovery and health benefits of travelling on foot in Britain and to promote respect for the life of the countryside.

Since its beginning in 1935, the work of the Ramblers has been in pursuit of its charitable aims: to encourage walking in Britain, to protect public paths, to campaign for freedom to roam over uncultivated country and to defend the beauty of the countryside.

Through more than 400 local groups, regular programmes of walks, climbs and other events are arranged throughout the year. There are more than 130 000 members in England, Wales and Scotland.

Members receive, as an entitlement, at no extra cost:

- An annual membership card
- An annual Yearbook and Accommodation Guide
- A quarterly colour magazine, The Rambler
- A quarterly newsletter, The Scottish Rambler
- Up to four newsletters a year
- Campaign information sheets on request

To apply for membership, contact the Membership Secretary of any of the local groups. Particulars in your local library or Ramblers Scotland, Auld Mart Business Park, Milnathort, Kinross KY13 9DA, phone 01577-861222, fax 01577-861333, email ramblersscot@sol.co.uk, web www.ramblers.org.uk/scotland

The Strathkelvin Group, publishers of this book, adjacent to other Groups: Bearsden and Milngavie; Cumbernauld and Kilsyth; Monklands; and Glasgow. Each has its separate programme of walks, published twice a year. The following is a brief extract from recent programmes to illustrate the wideranging nature of the organised events.

Grading of walks varies from group to group and standardisation is under discussion. Strathkelvin group adopt the following grades of walk:

A   Strenuous. Only for the fit. Often over high, rough terrain involving steep ascents/descents.

B+ Moderate to strenuous.

B   Moderate – hills and moorland paths.

C+ Mainly level but could have inclines – less than 17 km (10.5 miles).

C   Mainly level – less than 12 km (7.5 miles).

Strathkelvin Group, April 2001 – September 2001

Day	Month	Date	Grade	Location
Wed	Apr	4	C	Clachan of Campsie to Strathblane
Sat	"	7	B	The Whangie and Burncrooks Reservoir
Sat	"	14	B+	Trehenna Trip
Sat	"	21	B+	Coilessan Glen
"	"	"	B	Glen Loin
Thu	"	26		Social evening: Millennium Link slide show and talk
Sat	"	28	C+	Baldernock Circular
Wed	May	2	C	Chatelherault
Fri	"	4		
to Mon	"	7		Arran weekend
Sat	"	12	B	Ben Cleuch
"	"	12	C+	Tillicoultry Glen
Sat	"	19	B	Pentland Ridge
"	"	19	C+	Flotterstone to Threipmuir C.P.
Sat	"	26	C+	Crinan Canal
Sun	"	27	B	Menteith Hills
Sat	June	2	C	Walk followed by barbecue at Cashel
Sun	"	3	B+	Gleann an Dubh Choirein
Wed	"	6	C	Mugdock Circuit
Sat	"	9	A	Stob Ghabber
"	"	9	C+	Victoria Bridge circular
Sat	"	16	B	Findhu Glen (Glen Artney)
Sat	"	23	B	Bishop's Hill
Thu	"	28		Social evening. Walk at Palacerigg Country Park

Bearsden and Milngavie Group, November 2000 – April 2001

Day	Month	Date	Grade	Location
Tue	January	2		New Year Walk followed by pub lunch
Sat	"	6		Dungoil
Sat	"	13		Canal walk
Sun	"	14		Lyme Hill
Sat	"	20		Craigallian Loch circular
"	"	20		Strathclyde, Dumfries and Galloway AGM and walk
"	"	20		Panto night at King's Theatre
Sun	"	21		No leader, no walk
Fri	"	26		Burns Supper
Sat	"	27		Loch Lomond Woods
Sun	"	28		No leader, no walk
Sat	February	3		Coilessan Glen
Sun	"	4		Cameron Muir
Sat	"	10		Strathyre
Sun	"	11		No leader, no walk
Sat	"	17		Dumyat
Sun	"	18		Carron Valley Forest from Carron
Sat	"	24		Forth and Clyde Canal with pub lunch
Sun	"	25		No leader, no walk
Sat	March	3		Beinn Damhain
Sun	"	4		Stoneymollan from Balloch
Sat	"	10		Flanders Moss

Sun	"	11	No leader, no walk
Sat	"	17	Earl's Seat from Killearn
Sun	"	18	Balmaha to Drymen (WHW)
Sat	"	24	Cockleroy Hill and Beecraigs Country Park
Sun	"	25	Loch Ard
Sat	"	31	Creag A'Bhocain
"	"	31	Almondell and Calderwood Country Park

Cumbernauld and Kilsyth Group, April 2000 – August 2000

Day	Month	Date	Grade	Location
Sun	April	2	B+	Over Menteith Hills
"	"	2	B	Through Menteith Hills
Sun	"	9	B	Largo Bay to Pittenweem
Wed	"	12	C+	Culture walk in Falkirk
Thu	"	13		Social evening at the Smiddy Inn. Who dunnit? Mystery
Sun	"	16	A	Ben Chabhair
"	"	16	B	Lochan Beinn Chabhair
Sun	"	23	B	Meikle Bin
Wed	"	26	B	Glen Devon
Sun	"	30		Weekend walks for all
"	"	30	B	Dumyat circular
Sun	May	7	B	Kirkhouse (near Traquair) to St Mary's Loch
Wed	"	10	B	A walk in the Campsies
Thu	"	11		Social evening at the Smiddy Inn. Quiz night
Sun	"	14	A	Tweedsmuir to Culter via Culter Fell
"	"	14	B	Rachan Mill to Wolfclyde
Sun	"	21	A	Beinn Buidhe
"	"	21	C+	Ardrishaig to Crinan
Wed	"	24	C+	Helensburgh to Hill House
Sun	"	28	A	Ben Cleuch and King's Seat Hill
"	"	28	C+	Blair Logie to Dollar
Sun	June	4	A	Crieff to Comrie via Cairn Chois
"	"	4	B	Crieff to Comrie, missing out Cairn Chois
Wed	"	7	B	Garadhban Forest and Conic Hill, Balmaha
Thu	"	8		Social evening. Canal sail – Doon the watter
Sun	"	11	B	Aberfeldy to Kenmore
"	"	11	C+	Kenmore circular
Sun	"	18	C	Family ramble and fun day
Wed	"	21	C+	Trip to Younger Botanic Gardens, public transport
Sun	"	25	B	Glen Farg to Newburgh
"	"	6	B	Cockburnspath to Grantshouse
Thu	"	10		Social evening. Treasure trail
Sun	"	13	B	Grey Mare's Tail and Loch Skeen
Wed	"	16	B	Bonaly Country Park
Sun	"	20	A	A'Chrois and Ben Narnain
"	"	20	C	Inverbeg to Arrochar
Sun	"	27	B	Isle of Cumbrae
Wed	"	30	C	Chatelherault

151

Monklands Group, 8 October 2000 – 8 April 2001

Day	Month	Date	Grade	Location
Sun	October	8	B	Blackford to Tillicoultry
Sat	"	14	B	Strachur to Lochgoilhead
Sun	"	22	C+	Loch Na Craig circular
Sat	"	28	A+	Ben Lui
"	"	28	C+	Inveroran to Tyndrum
Sun	November	5	B+	Glen Ogle Cottage circular
Mon	"	6		Monklands Ramblers AGM
Sat	"	18	C+	Gateside to Freuchie
Sun	December	3	A+	Ben Vorlich (Loch Lomond)
"	"	3	B	Gleann nan Caorann
Sat	January	6	B	Arthur's Seat and Holyrood Park
Sat	"	13	B	Falls of Monzie to Glenturret (Crieff)
Sat	"	20		New Year ceilidh
Sun	"	28	A	Ben Vane (Balquidder)
"	"	28	B	Above Callander
Sat	February	3	A+	Ben Ime
"	"	3	B	Lochgoilhead to Ardgarten
Sun	"	18	B+	Tinto Hill
Sat	March	3	A+	Meall Greigh and Meall Garbh
"	"	3	B	Lochearnhead to Killin
Sun	"	18	B	Peebles to Innerleithen
Sat	"	31	C	North Queensferry to Boness via the Forth Bridge
Sun	April	8	A+	Beinn Dubhcraig and Ben Oss

Glasgow Group, November 2000 – April 2001

Day	Month	Date	Grade	Location
Sat	February	3	SC	Broughton Heights
Sat	"	10	SC	Overtoun House at Milton
Fri	"	16		Aladdin Ballet at the Theatre Royal
Sat	"	17	SC	Newton to Blantyre
Sat	"	24	SC	Historic Stirling
Sat	March	3	SA	Glas Maol and Creag Leacach
"	"	3	SC+	Bridge of Weir to Kilmacolm
Sat	"	10	SC	Campsie Right of Way walk
Sun	"	18	SA	Beinn an Lochain
Sat	"	24	SB+	Beinn Tharsuinn and Beinn Chaorach (from Glen Fruin)
Tue	"	27		Rigoletto – Opera on a Shoestring
Sat	"	31	SC	Strathblane circular
Sun	April	8	SA	Ben Donich
Sun	"	21	SB	Beinn Uamha
Sat	"	28	SC	Drymen
Sun	"	29	SB	Pentland Hills

The names and addresses of current office bearers for each Group are published in the annual Yearbook, but as these change from time to time it is advised to consult the most up-to-date literature in local libraries.

Tips for happy feet

Rachael Bryett explains the easy steps to healthy feet

OUR FEET carry us the equivalent of five times round the earth in an average lifetime, but we rarely give them the attention they deserve.

Each foot consists of 26 bones, supported by a network of ligaments and muscles. The feet, along with our eyes and hands, do more work than most parts of our body, so it's hardly surprising that things sometimes go wrong. Feet can also mirror general health – signs of diabetes and arthritis as well as circulatory and neurological disease often appear first in the feet.

Walking itself is good for the feet – it helps the muscles and ligaments work more efficiently and keeps them supple and flexible. Despite the stresses and strains that we place on them, our feet are highly adaptable and can withstand a lot of pressure before they rebel. Whether you walk a lot, or are planning a one-off walking trip, follow the following tips recommended by the Society of Chiropodists and Podiatrists:

1. Wash your feet regularly with soap and warm water, dry thoroughly (especially between the toes) and remove hard skin gently with pumice stone.
2. Trim your toenails straight across – not down the sides, as this can lead to ingrowing toenails.
3. Choose the right shoes for walking. With the foot pushed back against the heel of the shoe there should be a centimetre of room between the tip of your longest toe and the end of the shoe. Another test is to make sure you can just fit your little finger down the back of your heel. Shoes should be wide enough to allow the toes to move freely and deep enough so they don't push against the upper part of the shoe.
4. All walking shoes should have lace-up fastenings to keep the heel firmly in place. This helps prevent blisters and stop the toes slipping forward (particularly important when walking downhill).
5. Leather uppers mould well to the shape of your foot, are hard wearing and allow the foot to breathe, reducing sweating. Modern synthetic uppers such as Gore-Tex are also light and flexible, and remarkably efficient at keeping water out, while allowing feet to breathe.
6. Soles should be tough and long-lasting (usually synthetic) to offer both protection and grip. The tread should be deep enough to grip well in mud, and stop you wasting energy sliding around. In general, the deeper the tread, the better the grip.
7. As well as natural fibre socks, there are some superb synthetic fibres designed to keep sweat away from the skin and reduce the risk of blisters. A good idea is to wear two pairs of socks – a wicking liner sock to remove sweat from the skin, keeping it dry and so less likely to blister, and a second sock which provides extra padding.
8. Care for your shoes by cleaning and polishing them regularly. If they get wet, stuff them with newspaper and allow them to dry before using them again.

If you have problems with your feet it's best to seek professional help. The Society of Chiropodists and Podiatrists will be able to give you a list of registered chiropodists. Visit www.feetforlife.org, email enq@scpod.org or telephone 020 7234 8620.

This article first appeared in *The Rambler*, summer 2001, and is reproduced with the approval of the Editor.

Glasgow Natural History Society

Introducing the Society

The history of the Society dates from 1851; in that year the Natural History Society of Glasgow was founded by a few "gentlemen interested in the pursuit of Natural Science". In 1931 the Society united with the Andersonian Naturalists' Society founded in 1885 by members of a botany class in Anderson's College (now the University of Strathclyde) and with the Microscopical Society of Glasgow founded in 1886. The Society was renamed The Andersonian Naturalists of Glasgow and in 1979 became the Glasgow Natural History Society, a registered charity.

Under the guidance of a Council of some 20 members, the Society arranges a full programme of events throughout the year in Glasgow and district and occasionally further afield. These are at both specialist and semi-popular levels, designed to bring together the amateur and the professional –the expert and the beginner.

The Society is in close touch with various national bodies such as the Botanical Society of the British Isles, The Botanical society of Scotland, Scottish Natural Heritage and the Scottish Wildlife Trust. Members take part in national projects, for example the collection of data for the Atlas of the British Flora, and more general biological recording on both local and national scales. In alternate years, the Society collaborates with the BSBI Committee for Scotland in a half-day botanical conference in Glasgow.

The Society usually meets in the Graham Kerr Building, University of Glasgow, and has close co-operation with that University, with Glasgow Art Gallery and Museum at Kelvingrove, and with the University of Strathclyde.

Activities

The Glasgow Natural History Society:

Publishes

The Glasgow Naturalist, which includes papers on natural history, particularly of the Clyde area; short notes on local plants, birds, animals and rocks; and Proceedings of the Society, giving a summary of the meetings of the past year.

Arranges

- Indoor meetings, usually on the second Tuesday of each month (except July and August) to hear lectures from speakers from far and near, to exhibit specimens provided by members and others, and to bring naturalists and others together socially
- Tutorials on various aspects of natural history, held prior to most of the indoor meetings
- Outdoor meetings, usually between April and October on certain evenings, half days, full days and weekends, to study all aspects of natural history in the field with specialists, and to visit places of interest such as botanic gardens and research institutes

Maintains
- Sectional committees that organise activities for members interested in botany, zoology, geology, nature photography and relevant aspects of computing. Some of these activities cater particularly to beginners.
- A library of over 800 volumes, most of which may be borrowed in accordance with simple regulations. This is kept up to date by regular acquisitions, and journals are exchanged with over 30 other natural history societies in the UK.
- A number of microscopes, which are available for the use of members.

Privileges of membership
Members receive free:
- The Glasgow Naturalist
- Regular newsletters announcing meetings and giving Society and other news
- Syllabus of winter meetings
- Summer excursion programmes

Members can attend:
- Lectures, tutorials, discussions, visits and field excursions

Members can consult and borrow:
- Books from the Society Library, presently housed in the Graham Kerr Building, Glasgow University

Members can submit:
- Specimens for naming and for exhibition at meetings
- Queries on natural history topics
- Notes and papers for publication
- Photographs, slides and films for showing at meetings

Categories of membership

There is no entrance fee. Annual subscription rates are:

Ordinary, £17.00 – open to all; full privileges as set out above.

Family, £3.00 extra – open to spouses of ordinary members. Cannot vote or serve on Council and do not receive The Glasgow Naturalist or individual circulars.

Concessionary, £8.00 – open to those under 21, also full-time students and the unemployed. Full privileges.

School, £1.00 – open to school pupils (or pre-school). Cannot vote, serve on Council, or use the library, and do not receive the Glasgow Naturalist.

How to join

Any person wishing to become a member should contact the Membership Secretary, Glasgow Natural History Society, Art Gallery & Museum, Kelvingrove, Glasgow G3 8AG, for an application form.

The Royal Society for the Protection of Birds

The old district of Strathkelvin offers many opportunities to experience the bird life of Scotland. From the rolling Campsie Fells south towards Glasgow, the diverse habitats of woodlands, riverbanks and wetland areas are host to a wonderful variety of avian species.

The many riverbanks and lochs of Strathkelvin provide ideal habitat for Scotland's ducks and river songbirds. A winter walk along the Forth and Clyde Canal offers views of coots, moorhens and possibly goosanders with goldeneyes occasionally making an appearance. The fortunate walker may spot the electric blue plumage of the kingfisher, in search of an ideal fishing site. Dippers are quite common along the River Kelvin throughout the year. These small passerines may be seen dashing along the water's edge or foraging underwater for aquatic invertebrates and small fish. The unmistakable grey wagtail may also be spotted perched on a rock along the Kelvin, frequently dashing out after passing insects. Frankfield Loch is a must in spring to see the graceful courtship display of the great crested grebes. In July, the Loch offers great views of these birds ferrying their stripey young around on their back, to keep them safe from harm. Little grebes nest among the reeds and vegetation on both Frankfield Loch and Hogganfield Loch and can be seen with their young during July and August. Reed beds on the lochs are equally ideal for whitethroats, willow warblers and a growing number of reed buntings, which have benefited from recent habitat management by Kelvin Valley Projects.

Upland regions of the Strathkelvin district are excellent for short rambles, with wonderful views of the Kelvin floodplain and resident wildlife. The open landscape and patchy heather cover of the Campsie Fells represent ideal feeding grounds for birds of prey. Peregrines nest in the hills, performing their aerial courtship displays during April and May. Buzzards, more common in recent years, are regularly seen soaring high on thermal vents. Vigilant kestrels hover in flight, watching for voles or mice in the ground cover below. Waders, such as common sandpiper, can be found near rivers and lochs, with curlew nesting in the heather cover of semi-upland areas. In late autumn, short-eared owls glide silently in search of prey over open areas. The crags around Hart Hill represent a particularly important area for twite. These small upland birds, also known as the "mountain linnet", are often overlooked, owing to their less than striking appearance. They nest in small groups in open areas and their distinct pink rump serves as an identification feature when seen in flight.

Farmland habitat provides ideal feeding and breeding opportunities for many birds. In Scotland, lapwing numbers have fallen considerably in recent years, yet these birds breed in good numbers near Twechar Marsh, feeding in the neighbouring fields. Redshank and snipe also breed at the marsh, with the occasional whimbrel seen on spring passage. The ideal wetland habitat of the marsh attracts garganey, shelduck and possibly ruff during the summer months. Winter brings the occasional pintail, en route from Greenland to warmer southern climes. Just 4 km west of Twechar, the wetland SSSI (Site of Special Scientific Interest) of Dullator Marsh is teaming with warblers, wildfowl and winter waders. Breeding water rail, teal and snipe make this a particularly important ornithological site.

A summer visit is a rewarding experience. The song of yellow hammer, whinchat and whitethroat can clearly be heard and the canal path offers great views of the birds in the marsh. In late autumn, the ever-illusive jacksnipe may be glimpsed amidst the wetland vegetation of the marsh.

Undoubtedly, the Strathkelvin area supports a great diversity of birds and other wildlife. The proximity of Strathkelvin to large urban conurbations also makes it a valuable leisure and recreational resource. Recent regeneration of the Forth and Clyde Canal has improved access to the area, leaving Strathkelvin and its natural beauty open to all.

RSPB Scotland works for a healthy environment rich in birds and other wildlife. We depend on the support and generosity of others to make a difference. If you would like to support our work, please join the Society.

For further details about RSPB Scotland, please contact us:

Tel: 0141 576 2610

email: glasgow@rspb.org.uk

website: http://www.rspb.org.uk

Scottish Wildlife Trust

Founded in 1964, the Scottish Wildlife Trust (SWT) is an independent membership organisation and a national charity. It is the only voluntary body that enhances and conserves the whole of the natural environment and wildlife of Scotland.

The SWT seeks to work with people from all sections of society to engender a lasting interest in and commitment to wildlife. Its work covers a range of interrelated areas, from conservation to lifelong learning. Working closely with members and volunteers, the SWT seeks to promote the protection, enjoyment and understanding of Scotland's wildlife and natural environment.

Within Scotland, the SWT also works in partnership with a range of organisations including Scottish Natural heritage, the Scottish Environmental Protection Agency and, in particular, over 30 other environmental non-governmental organisations which together comprise the Scottish Environment LINK.

In the broader context of the UK, the SWT works in collaboration with a network of 46 other wildlife trusts. Together the trusts represent 350 000 members, manage over 2300 wildlife reserves and give wildlife a louder voice throughout the UK and beyond.

How the SWT is organised

The SWT's Council of Trustees provides strategic direction and the formulation of policy for the Trust. The implementation of SWT policies is the responsibility of a management board and chief executive who are responsible for overseeing the Trust's programmes, working with over 100 full-time staff throughout Scotland. The SWT's main office is in Edinburgh, while the three regional offices are in Glasgow (West region), Inverness (North region) and Stirling (East region).

For more information

For more information about the SWT and how you can support them through membership or volunteering, contact Helen Corget, Membership Development Manager on 0131 312 4750 or hcorbet@swt.org.uk

Scottish Wildlife Trust
Cramond House
Kirk Cramond
Cramond Glebe Road
Edinburgh EH4 6NS

Email: membership@swt.org.uk
Tel: 0131 312 7765
www.swt.org.uk

Sustrans

Sustrans (Sustainable Transport) works on practical projects to encourage people to cycle and walk more, as a starting point for reducing motor traffic and tackling its adverse effects.

The flagship project, the National Cycle Network, which started as the germ of an idea in the 1980s, opened 5000 miles of on-road and traffic-free routes in the summer of 2000. Other projects include Safe Routes to Schools, Bike to Work and the extension of the network to 10 000 miles by 2005.

Safer signed routes are a new concept to help the commuter cyclist and encourage more people to travel for short journeys by cycle. These consist of well marked and signed routes on minor roads, footways and cycle tracks, specifically chosen so that the cyclist is guided through areas with less traffic. Where the route uses a major road, this is usually in the context of a specially provided lane or track, and is often in a traffic-calmed sector. It is hoped that these routes will enable commuters to take to the bike in more safety and with greater speed and comfort, and, as a bonus, help to reduce congestion of the roads at the same time.

There is a monthly magazine, National Cycle Magazine, the official guide to the National Cycle Network and a range of recommended Guides.

Routes that are of particular relevance to readers of this book are:

The towpath of the Forth and Clyde Canal

This is fully described in a preceding chapter.

The Clyde Walkway

This is an almost completely off-road link from Glasgow to Strathclyde Park. It also forms the western section of the Glasgow to Edinburgh Cycle Route. It starts at the Scottish Exhibition and Conference Centre, near where the Garden Festival was held, an area now being dramatically redeveloped. This is also the starting point of the Glasgow to Loch Lomond and Killin Cycleway heading west out of the city, and the route through Paisley to Irvine southwards.

The Cumbernauld to Glasgow Safer Signed Route

The route starts on the south-west side of Cumbernauld, using signs to denote safer, minor roads until Muirhead is reached. After Muirhead, the route uses the specifically widened footway along the A80 as a cycle track to the east end of Stepps, where on-road cycle lanes have been designated and surfaced. This is one feature of the extensive traffic-calming scheme here, started after the completion of the M80 Stepps bypass. When Millerston is reached, existing roads are used, including cycle lanes in traffic-calming cycle tracks on widened footways. Finally, the route goes over Sighthill Road and through Sighthill Park, going over the M8 by footbridge and straight down to the city centre.

The Kirkintilloch to Strathblane Cycle Route
This picturesque route that uses the Gartness to Kirkintilloch railway has been described earlier as part of the Strathkelvin Railway Walkway, and was also mentioned when describing the route to join the West Highland Way.

In addition to the wealth of information contained in Sustrans publications, other recommended books are:

25 Walkways Around Glasgow, by Alan Forbes, HMSO
25 Cycle Routes In and Around Glasgow, by E.B. Wilkie, HMSO
A Hundred Hill Walks Around Glasgow, by John Chalmers, Mainstream Publishing
Glasgow's Pathways, by E.B. Wilkie, Mainstream Publishing

Sustrans can be reached at: 162 Fountainbridge, Edinburgh EH3 9RX.
Telephone: 0131 624 7660; Fax: 0131 624 7664.

Scottish Rights of Way & Access Society

The Society's history, role and function

The Scottish Rights of Way & Access Society was founded in 1845 by Lord Provost Adam Black of Edinburgh, in response to the progressive enclosure of the open country around Edinburgh and the consequent loss of recreational opportunities. The initial vision was only for Edinburgh.

In 1847, the Society's vision expanded to embrace the whole of Scotland, following a watershed court case concerning Glen Tilt, which was successfully contested against the Duke of Atholl. A second *cause célèbre* followed in 1887, when the Jock's Road path from Angus to Depside was the subject of another landmark case, again won by the Society. Both these cases were pursued all the way to the House of Lords.

Throughout the mid- and late Victorian era – the heyday of the sporting estate – the Society sought to signpost all the major long-distance traditional routes in the Highlands, so as to secure these for the small, but growing, body of walkers and climbers.

In 1884, James Brace MP introduced his "Access to the Mountains" Bill to Parliament. Though it was never enacted, he was 100 years ahead of his time! In 1894, Westminster passed the "Local Government Scotland" Act, which gave new powers to the local authorities to assert, protect and keep open public rights of way. The Society was ready to disband, on the basis that its life work was done and would now be taken over by the local authorities. However, the weakness of the new Act was that the powers conferred were only discretionary, rather than obligatory.

From that day to this, the Society has acted as a "citizens' advice bureau" relating to recreational access to the countryside, advising both countryside "hosts" and countryside "visitors" as to their rights under planning and Rights of Way law. A major part of the Society's effort goes into trouble-shooting – i.e. the investigation of path problems.

The Society now has a day-to-day working relationship with all the other major players in the field, primarily the Access Forum, Scottish Natural Heritage (SNH), Forest Enterprise, all 32 local authorities, the Paths For All Partnership, *sportscotland*, the National Farmers' Union, the Scottish Landowners' Federation, Community Councils plus clubs and organisations representing a wide range of recreational activities.

In recent years, the Society has participated in the National Access Forum, preparing the ground for the Scottish Parliament's Land Reform Bill, which will include a "new deal" regarding recreation in the countryside – just as James Brace was seeking in 1884!

The society holds the master-copy of the National Catalogue of Rights of Way, which is shared with SNH and all local authorities. The Society's members are walking every listed route and compiling descriptions of each, in order to augment the Catalogue.

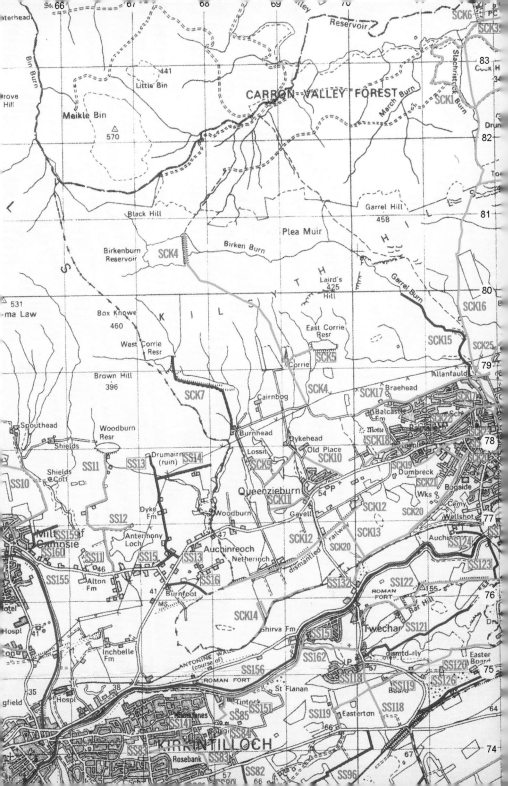

The Society's most visible face is its network of familiar green and white signs, which extends from Sutherland to the Solway and from Mull to the Merse. Their style has evolved over the decades, but the basic white lettering on a green background remains constant and has become the national norm, as used by the majority of local authorities and other organisations. The same signs are now used for all types of path, in addition to rights of way, reflecting the Society's expanded role to include all access matters.

Financial support comes not only from subscriptions – individual and corporate – but also from the Scottish Executive, as well as from local authorities, SNH and community groups for specific on-the-ground projects. The Society is supported by over 2000 individual members and by over 200 corporate members, including most of Scotland's Community Councils and local authorities, many history and amenity groups and a range of recreational clubs. This broad support represents the Society's mandate to represent all and every type of countryside user.

The Society organises a programme of walks throughout the year.

The Society is always delighted to welcome new supporters and activists. For an application form for either yourself or your organisation, please contact The Scottish Rights of Way and Access Society, 24 Annandale Street, Edinburgh EH7 4AN (telephone and fax 0131 558 1222; email srws@scotways.demon.co.uk; website www.scotways.demon.co.uk).

National Catalogue of Rights of Way & Other Routes (CROW)

Copyright. Base data on these maps is the copyright of Ordnance Survey but the overlying CROW data is the joint copyright of Scottish Natural Heritage (SNH) and the Scottish Rights of Way and Access Society (ScotWays).

Routes. The routes shown on the map have been prepared from information contained in the records of ScotWays, in those local authorities and in judicial and other records. The representation of any particular route infers no claim on the part of ScotWays as to its legal status. Many are believed to be public rights of way but not all rights of way are shown.

Enquiries. All enquiries and comments should be sent in writing to the National Secretary, ScotWays, 24 Annandale Street, Edinburgh EH7 4AN.

Maps – © Crown Copyright. All rights reserved. ScotWays Licence Number AL 100011826.

CROW data – © Copyright ScotWays ® / SNH. All rights reserved. Reproduction not permitted without prior approval from ScotWays, 24 Annandale Street, Edinburgh EH7 4AN, Scotland.

Scottish Rights of Way & Access Society
List of footpaths in Strathkelvin

SROWS

number	Name	From	To	km
SS1	–	NS 613 800	NS 629 799	1.6
SS2	Campsie Glen	NS 611795	NS 623 807	2
SS3	St Machans Well – Crow Road	NS 611797	NS 613 800	0.4
SS4	–	NS 609 795	NS 610 791	0.4
SS5	–	NS 611 795	NS 610 793	1.8
SS6	–	NS 606 790	NS 600 797	0.9
SS7	Dukeston Turnoff	NS 604 789	NS 596 796	1.2
SS8	Lennoxtown High Park	NS 630 779	NS 627 785	0.7
SS9	Double Hedges	NS 641 771	NS 633 780	1.7
SS10	Glorat–Craighead	NS 643 771	NS 653 768	2
SS11	Woodburn Reservoir via Antermony Loch	NS 665 779	NS 667 763	2
SS12	–	NS 665 769	NS 669 770	0.4
SS13	–	NS 672 779	NS 676 765	1.3
SS14	–	NS 672 776	NS 680 777	0.8
SS15	–	NS 674 765	NS 673 764	0.25
SS16	–	NS 674 761	NS 679 760	0.5
SS17	Hillside Terrace – Muckcroft, incl. Nappie Loan	NS 634 766 NS 634 766	NS 648 764 NS 648 764	1.3 1.3
SS18	Viewfield Cottage – Kincaird Hotel	NS 647 764	NS 649 760	0.4
SS19	Birdston – Campsie Road "Cat Walk"	NS 654 753	NS 638 754	1.5
SS20	Kinkell – nr. Acre Valley Road	NS 634 759	NS 619 767	3
SS21	Mealybrae – Station Road	NS 598 751	NS 625 776	4.5
SS22	Acre Valley Road – Blairskaith	NS 619 762	NS 604 762	1.5
SS23	Mealybrae to Fluchter Rd	NS 598 758	NS 591 758	0.8
SS24	–	NS 625 776	NS 630 773	0.5
SS25	–	NS 619 764	NS 630 773	1.5
SS26	–	NS 581 753	NS 582 760	0.7
SS27	–	NS 568 756	NS 575 757	0.8
SS28	–	NS 576 749	NS 577 750	0.3

number	Name	From	To	km
SS29	–	NS 582 740	NS 583 747	0.5
SS30	–	NS 587 736	NS 584 745	0.8
SS31	–	NS 585 743	NS 584 742	0.2
SS32	–	NS 596 735	NS 588 747	1.4
SS33	–	NS 599 746	NS 593 742	0.8
SS34	–	NS 599 748	NS 597 747	0.25
SS35	–	NS 614 748	NS 607 750	0.7
SS36	–	NS 610 753	NS 608 761	0.8
SS37	–	NS 618 750	NS 614 758	1
SS38	–	NS 622 755	NS 622 747	1
SS39	–	NS 622 748	NS 627 746	0.4
SS40	Craigen Glen Cottage	NS 623 750	NS 626 748	0.3
SS41	–	NS 622 746	NS 618 747	0.3
SS42	–	NS 618 744	NS 611 742	0.7
SS43	–	NS 624 744	NS 627 741	0.3
SS44	–	NS 630 748	NS 634 741	0.8
SS45	Bardowie Station Area	NS 583 734	NS 583 734	1
SS46	Balmore Haughs	NS 590 736	NS 602 734	2.1
SS47	–	NS 594 731	NS 598 730	0.7
SS48	–	NS 616 723	NS 604 734	1.8
SS49	Buchley Cottages	NS 590 720	NS 590 724	0.5
SS50	Wilderness Plantation	NS 599 720	NS 600 715	0.6
SS51	Cadder Golf Club – Canal Towpath	NS 615 722	NS 615 722	3
SS52	Cadder Golf Club	NS 602 726	NS 607 726	0.6
SS53	–	NS 610 718	NS 610 722	0.4
SS54	–	NS 629 711	NS 635 718	1.2
SS55	–	NS 594 709	NS 617 721	2.5
SS56	–	NS 614 719	NS 616 718	0.3
SS57	–	NS 616 719	NS 613 718	0.2
SS58	–	NS 613 718	NS 614 717	0.2
SS59	Bishopbriggs Burn Path	NS 600 714	NS 610 704	1.4
SS60	(Number no longer used)			
SS61	–	NS 632 698	NS 628 702	0.8
SS62	–	NS 605 699	NS 602 699	0.3
SS63	–	NS 602 702	NS 597 702	0.6
SS64	St Mary's Road Loop	NS 601 706	NS 599 706	0.6
SS65	–	NS 634 729	NS 632 722	0.8

number	Name	From	To	km
SS66	Ladies Mile	NS 655 718	NS 644 714	1.2
SS67	–	NS 621 739	NS 641 742	2.2
SS68	–	NS 642 743	NS 645 745	0.3
SS69	–	NS 650 734	NS 649 736	0.2
SS70	–	NS 655 710	NS 657 705	0.6
SS71	Lenzie Golf Club	NS 657 707	NS 658 707	0.1
SS72	Langmuirhead Road –Play-ing Fields "The Neuk"	NS 658 705	NS 660 707	0.6
SS73	Spiders Bridge	NS 664 726	NS 671 730	1
SS74	–	NS 662 722	NS 669 718	0.9
SS75	–	NS 666 718	NS 674 718	0.9
SS76	–	NS 672 734	NS 676 732	0.5
SS77	–	NS 677 731	NS 677 728	0.4
SS78	–	NS 678 731	NS 682 728	0.6
SS79	–	NS 678 731	NS 682 728	0.6
SS80	–	NS 679 733	NS 685 735	0.5
SS81	–	NS 679 734	NS 679 736	0.2
SS82	–	NS 684 735	NS 684 738	0.3
SS83	–	NS 679 738	NS 671 740	1
SS84	–	NS 683 740	NS 681 742	0.3
SS85	Tintock	NS 681 742	NS 681 746	0.4
SS86	–	NS 685 723	NS 691 720	0.4
SS87	Stoneyetts	NS 691 718	NS 696 712	0.8
SS88	–	NS 693 717	NS 700 718	0.7
SS89	Bridgend "Bow Wow"	NS 687 705	NS 691 707	0.5
SS90	Bridgend "Bow Wow"	NS 691 707	NS 691 709	0.2
SS91	Hill of Chryston "Pit Brae"	NS 677 710	NS 687 707	1
SS92	Hill of Chryston "Pit Brae"	NS 687 707	NS 688 712	0.5
SS93	–	NS 673 697	NS 679 698	0.6
SS94	–	NS 672 690	NS 667 701	1.2
SS95	Hornshill	NS 657 692	NS 664 690	1.2
SS96	–	NS 690 733	NS 702 742	1.6
SS97	Auchengree	NS 653 700	NS 656 695	0.8
SS98	Whitehill Farm Road (N)	NS 655 685	NS 653 689	0.5
SS99	Whitehill Farm Road (S)	NS 655 685	NS 650 684	0.6
SS100	Garnkirk "School Path" or "Irish Path"	NS 663 683	NS 683 683	1.7

number	Name	From	To	km
SS101	Heathfield Moss "Heathfield Path"	NS 681 685	NS 684 692	1
SS102	Garnkirk "School Path" or "Irish Path"	NS 680 680	NS 681 685	0.6
SS103	Garnkirk "School Path" or "Irish Path"	NS 676 683	NS 680 680	0.5
SS104	Moss Path	NS 683 692	NS 684 691	0.2
SS105	Slakiewood "Lees Walk"	NS 689 691	NS 688 695	0.5
SS106	–	NS 695 696	NS 691 696	0.7
SS107	–	NS 693 695	NS 694 692	0.5
SS108	Bedlay "Wellbrae"	NS 690 701	NS 696 700	0.6
SS109	Strathkelvin Railway Walkway	NS 656 730	NS 677 716	1.8
SS110	–	NS 659 725	NS 659 728	0.3
SS111	–	NS 687 683	NS 690 681	0.7
SS112	Gartcosh Station "Smith & Mclean Road"	NS 699 678	NS 704 676	0.5
SS113	Croftfoot "Ducks Walk"	NS 700 681	NS 710 684	1.3
SS114	Mollinhead to Cumbernauld Road	NS 717 715	NS 712 710	0.7
SS115	–	NS 719 712	NS 720 704	0.8
SS116	–	NS 708 728	NS 709 733	0.5
SS117	–	NS 709 736	NS 708 734	0.3
SS118	–	NS 701 751	NS 704 742	0.9
SS119	Easterton	NS 697 742	NS 707 750	1.5
SS120	–	NS 708 750	NS 720 754	1.5
SS121	–	NS 701 752	NS 716 758	1.6
SS122	Twechar to Roman Fort	NS 701 757	NS 721 762	2.2
SS123	–	NS 719 767	NS 719 762	0.5
SS124	–	NS 717 767	NS 714 768	0.3
SS125	–	NS 711 730	NS 709 730	0.2
SS126	–	NS 708 744	NS 717 750	1
SS127	Turner's Road	NS 622 742	NS 624 740	0.4
SS128	–	NS 601 741	NS 607 735	0.9
SS129	–	NS 699 712	NS 700 710	0.3
SS130	Hayston Farm	NS 643 740	NS 642 746	1
SS131	–	NS 647 746	NS 648 752	0.9
SS132	Twechar – Kilsyth	NS 699 761	NS 701 764	0.4

number	Name	From	To	km
SS133	–	NS 623 732	NS 635 730	1.3
SS134	–	NS 673 747	NS 668 746	0.8
SS135	–	NS 683 730	NS 688 734	0.7
SS136	–	NS 683 730	NS 691 731	0.9
SS137	–	NS 646 733	NS 644 735	0.5
SS138	–	NS 616 696	NS 613 969	0.3
SS139	–	NS 614 715	NS 615 714	0.2
SS140	–	NS 617 712	NS 618 710	0.3
SS141	–	NS 676 741	NS 675 742	0.3
SS142	Lenzie Moss Tracks	NS 654 719	NS 647 722	0.8
SS143	–	NS 611 795	NS 626 786	2
SS144	–	NS 619 785	NS 620 786	0.2
SS145	Glazertbank Field	NS 630 772	NS 632 773	0.3
SS146	–	NS 627 786	NS 630 779	1.1
SS147	Loch Road, Stepps	NS 655 682	NS 660 678	0.6
SS148	Well Lane	NS 628 777	NS 627 776	0.2
SS149	–	NS 624 744	NS 622 747	0.3
SS150	–	NS 680 694	NS 680 693	0.1
SS151	–	NS 693 756	NS 682 746	1.5
SS152	–	NS 636 771	NS 638 765	0.7
SS153	–	NS 717 716	NS 718 712	0.5
SS154	Wilderness Plantation	NS 594 710	NS 604 719	1.6
SS155	Strathkelvin Railway Walkway	NS 581 787	NS 656 743	10
SS156	Forth & Clyde Towpath	NS 594 710	NS 718 767	15
SS157	Railway Walkway, Red Moss	NS 643 765	NS 644 768	0.4
SS158	–	NS 679 704	NS 671 706	0.8
SS159	Craighead Field	NS 653 766	NS 659 770	0.6
SS160	–	NS 655 767	NS 658 767	0.3
SS161	–	NS 640 735	NS 639 737	0.3
SS162	Shirva Glen	NS 692 753	NS 700 753	0.8
SS163	–	NS 596 738	NS 600 737	0.6
SS164	–	NS 677 328	NS 677 318	0.1
SS165	–	NS 655 712	NS 655 710	0.2
SS166	–	NS 691 720	NS 686 717	0.3
SS167	Strathkelvin Railway Walkway	NS 677 716	NS 702 696	3.2

Scottish Natural Heritage

Scottish Natural Heritage is a government body established by Parliament in 1992, responsible to the Secretary of State for Scotland.

Our task is to secure the conservation and enhancement of Scotland's unique and precious natural heritage – the wildlife, the habitats and the landscapes which have evolved in Scotland through the long partnership between people and nature.

We advise on policies and promote projects that aim to improve the natural heritage and support its sustainable use.

Our aim is to help people enjoy Scotland's natural heritage responsibly, understand it more fully and use it wisely so that it can be sustained for future generations.

Further copies of this code are available from
Publications Section, Scottish Natural Heritage,
Battleby, Redgorton, Perth PH1 3EW

The Country Code

- **Enjoy the countryside and respect its life and work**
  Help those who live and work in the countryside by being a careful and considerate visitor, and by following the Country Code. A courteous and friendly approach to all you meet will help us all enjoy the countryside better.
- **Guard against all risk of fire**
  Accidental fire is a great fear of farmers and foresters. Be careful to put out all used cigarettes and matches, and cook by stove rather than by fire. Be especially careful during dry periods, and never throw a cigarette out of a car window.
- **Leave all gates as you find them**
  But if you find a gate closed, always make sure that you leave it closed, to avoid farm animals straying. Farmers sometimes leave gates open to allow their animals to graze in the next field or to get water. So help a farmer by leaving gates as you find them but, if in doubt, do close a gate.
- **Keep your dogs under close control**
  Always keep your dog on a lead when walking on roads or when close to farm animals. Your dog may be well behaved, but the farmer does not know this. At other times always keep your dog under close control so as not to disturb wildlife, or annoy or alarm other visitors.
- **Keep to paths across farmland**
  Avoid damage to growing crops by walking around the edge of fields or by keeping to an existing path across it. Avoid entering fields with farm animals, especially where there are young animals, and if you are with a dog.
- **Use gates and stiles to cross fences, hedges and walls**
  Damage to a fence, wall or hedge can allow animals to get out, so help the farmer by using gates and stiles. If you must climb a gate because it is difficult to open, always do this at the hinged end.
- **Leave livestock and crops and machinery alone**
  Crops, animals and machinery are all of high value. Help the farmer, and care for your own safety too by not interfering with any equipment or animals – and don't let others do this.
- **Take your litter home**
  Broken glass, tins and plastic bags can be dangerous to people and farm animals, and wildlife can also be trapped and die. All litter is unsightly so always take yours, and any that you come across, home with you to dispose of properly.
- **Help keep all water clean**
  Not everyone living in the countryside is on the public water supply, so take care with your personal hygiene to avoid causing any pollution. Farm animals need clean water too, so don't interfere with water troughs provided for livestock.

- **Protect wildlife, plants and trees**
  Leave all natural places as you find them. Never uproot plants as they'll be gone forever. If you come across wildlife, keep your distance and don't watch for too long lest you cause disturbance and stress, especially if adults are with young and in winter, when food may be scarce or weather harsh.
- **Take special care on country roads**
  Always drive with care and reduced speed on country roads. Park your car with consideration to others' needs, especially to avoid blocking gateways or other drivers' sight-lines. Walkers, particularly large groups, should take special care on country roads.
- **Make no unnecessary noise**
  People go to the countryside to enjoy its peace and quiet, so avoid noise or disruptive behaviour which might annoy residents or visitors, or frighten farm animals or wildlife.

The last word

Inevitably there are errors, which will no doubt be pointed out by readers without prompting. There are omissions. Readers are respectfully requested to send their favourite walks – narrated and illustrated – for inclusion with grateful acknowledgement in the next edition.